Uncle Jim,

Get after it!

GET AFTER IT

SEVEN INSPIRATIONAL STORIES
TO FIND YOUR INNER STRENGTH
WHEN IT MATTERS MOST

PARKER SCHAFFEL

Printed in the United States of America

First Printing, 2018

Print ISBN: 978-1-54393-528-8

eBook ISBN: 978-1-54393-529-5

www.parkerschaffel.com

To my wife, Abby, for her support,
and to my grandfather, Art, for his inspiration

"You are the driver, you own the road!
You are the fire, go on, explode!
You've got desire, so let it out!
You've got the power, stand up and shout!"

– Ronnie James Dio

TABLE OF CONTENTS

FOREWORD: SHARING MY STORIES

I remember the first poor grade I got in school. Mrs. Winkler's third grade English. I started out with a B, then fell to a C in the second quarter, continuing the downward trend with the lowest grade possible without failing—a D in the third quarter. To this day, I remember the conversation I had with my mom about it. She asked me, as confused as I felt, "What's going on? Why did you get this grade? What's happening?"

From a young age, I was better at math and science, thanks to my dad, the computer programmer who used to quiz me on multiplication tables when I was six and seven years old. English, and everything that went along with it, such as reading books, writing book reports, and the like, wasn't my strong suit. As I made my way through middle and high school, that inclination continued, and English was the only subject in which I wasn't in an advanced class. No AP English. No honors English. Just regular old English class for me.

When I went to college, I planned on being an engineer because that would give me the best shot at earning a scholarship through the Air Force Reserve Officer Training Corps (ROTC) program. To my surprise, the Air Force offered me a scholarship anyway, and told me I could pick any major I wanted. I wasn't keen on being an engineer, and because I really liked war movies and documentaries, I picked military history, thinking it would be a great fit for my passion and career goals, which included the military.

I earned an A in my first history class, and thought, *Hey, I can do this!* But I had a rude awakening a year later when my German history professor, Dr. Alan Beyerchen, assigned our class to write a paper on the major themes of the book *Rites of Spring* and relate them to the German geopolitical situation during the First World War, a daunting task regardless of the length of the paper. The problem was he wanted five pages or less. The task seemed impossible.

That paper was my first foray into *real* writing, not the fluff I had done before for term papers and essays. It made me think and write in ways I hadn't before and made me write more succinctly as well. Every word mattered. Although I only earned a B in the class, Dr. Beyerchen was the first teacher to push me that far, and he taught me something that would eventually change my life: I learned how to write.

When I started as a military analyst at the Central Intelligence Agency, writing became my life, as it is the key tenet of the job. Publish or perish not only applies to the journalism and literary worlds, but to intelligence analysis as well. From 2007 to 2010, I wrote dozens of papers on a variety of topics, doing the best I could in each one. While I actually enjoyed writing, my analysis suffered. I just wasn't as good as my coworkers at figuring out trends and making predictions.

Then, in 2010, a series of tragic events occurred within three weeks, including my first breakup of a long-term relationship, switching work schedules from a normal day schedule to working nights, and moving into a new place in which I lived alone. This confluence led me into the grief cycle for the first time in adulthood. During that time, I felt alone and distant from others, and I recognized that working a six-month stint on a night shift wasn't helping. I was able to find solace through one important task: journaling.

On a daily basis, I wrote about my feelings, which helped me process and move through the cycle. After I was done grieving, however, I didn't stop writing. I found myself continuing to write on a regular basis about anything and everything that impacted my life—my friends, my family, my job, my roommates—and other tangential subjects such as my views on politics, the millennial generation, sports, and my daily activities. I started to write and didn't stop. Even when I went overseas on long-term assignments, I kept a travel journal and emailed passages back to friends and family.

By 2017, I reviewed everything I had and was astonished. I had written more than 500 pages. But what was I going to do with them? What good were these words if not to be shared with others? What purpose did they have?

I decided I would publish them in a book, this book, and share my stories with the world. I reread everything and determined that I had seven stories that were the most meaningful and impactful in my life. These are the stories I share. Many of these stories cover several years, sometimes nine or even 10 years, and touch on both personal and professional situations in my life. Some are positive and uplifting, while another tells the tale of a serious blunder. Some of the stories may leave you in disbelief but inspired, while others, I hope, will provide the motivation to achieve your own goals, and as I say, "Get after it."

And in the end, that's what this book is all about. It's about telling the world how I get after life, and how, maybe, you can learn from my adventures, as well as my mistakes, to make your own life that much better.

Enjoy . . .

And get after it.

CHAPTER 1

NEVER GIVING UP: MY EIGHT-YEAR QUEST TO COMMISSION IN THE MILITARY

I grew up in Rockville, Maryland, a large suburb of Washington, D.C., and had lived there my entire young life, except for my first two years in which my mom and I lived in another suburb. It was a nice place to live. We had a small house to ourselves—the smallest in the neighborhood, in fact—and only later in life did I find out that it was because my mom qualified for the low-income program. As a child of a single parent, we didn't have much, but we were happy with what we had.

I was lucky to also have my grandparents close by, just a 30-minute drive around the D.C. beltway. My grandparents were younger than most other grandparents, as my grandmother had my mom when she was 20 years old, and my mom had me when she was 25. From my earliest memories, my grandfather, Art, was someone with whom I spent a lot of time. Simply put, he was a great man.

He grew up dirt poor in Brooklyn, New York, in the 1930s, spending much of his young life in foster homes. He had no father figure, and his mother didn't work. When he did live at home, he worked any job he could to earn money for food for his two brothers and one sister. Even though he was not the oldest sibling, he acted like it. He graduated from high school with high marks, thanks to his mentality that he professed his entire life: "If the average person can do something, then so can I, because I think I'm at least average."

In 1951, at 18 years of age and as a high school graduate, my grandfather enrolled in courses in Brooklyn College, until one day he received a letter in the mail. It was the U.S. Army. They wanted him for Korea. He went to the physical exam, as he was required to do, and had an interview with an Army psychologist.

"What do you think about the Army?" the psychologist asked.

"I don't," he said, as he stood up and walked out.

"If I had to fight a war, I didn't want to do it on the ground," he told me. "I wanted to be in the air." About a week later, my grandfather enlisted in the U.S. Air Force, and shortly after joining was selected for officer commissioning school. He spent the next 20 years of his life in the Air Force, navigating a B-47 bomber and KC-135 refueling aircraft, as well as analyzing intelligence. His missions took him to the edges of the world: combat bombing missions in Vietnam; refueling missions over the North Pole; and almost certainly deep missions into the Soviet Union, during which his aircraft might have been carrying nuclear weapons, a story he will neither confirm nor deny today at 85 years of age. "As far as I'm concerned, those missions are still classified," he said. "I wouldn't even tell the President."

While I'll never be certain as to the exact reason, whether it was simply spending a lot of time with him when I was younger, or because of the stories he told me, or the pictures I saw of him in his uniform, I wanted to follow in his footsteps. I wanted to be in the Air Force. I wanted to fly. While I didn't know much of anything when I was 17 years old, I knew I wanted to be in the air. I wanted to be an officer. I wanted to wear a uniform with ribbons, and medals, and rank . . . just like my hero, my grandfather.

To become an officer, I had to be a college graduate, which meant either attending the Air Force Academy or completing a four-year Air Force ROTC program at another school. Even though I went to Thomas Wootton High School, one of the top public high schools in the country, my grades were mediocre at best, and there was no way I was getting a nomination to any military academy. ROTC was my only option.

During my senior year of high school, I applied for an Air Force ROTC scholarship, but my application was denied. My grades just weren't good enough. And that wasn't the only denial I would get, as I applied to seven schools and was rejected from all of them: Maryland, Penn State, Miami, Towson, Syracuse, Florida, and Minnesota. Things were not looking bright.

One day in my Advanced Placement Physics class, I told a friend about my troubles.

"Dude, you should apply to Ohio State. There's no essay."

I went home that night, wrote up an application, and dropped it with the registrar the next day. As January turned into February, I still had no idea what my post-high school plans were going to be, and I was about four months from graduation. I applied to the University of Maine and Virginia Tech, just hoping someone would let me in. No college degree meant no officer commissioning program.

The second week in February, I received a letter from Ohio State: "Congratulations on your admission to Autumn Quarter 2002 at The Ohio State University's Columbus campus." I ran from the mailbox to our house and starting yelling for my mom.

"Mom! Mom! I'm going to college!" I screamed. She was on the phone with a friend.

"Oh, my god! Parker is going to college!" We celebrated that evening with a family dinner, all of us with smiles that I would be attending, somehow, a great academic institution. A few months later during my freshman orientation at Ohio State, I enrolled in Air Science 101, the beginning freshman class of Air Force ROTC, despite a lack of scholarship. It didn't matter to me. I'd earn a scholarship. I had my dream.

As our new freshmen class sat in a classroom in Converse Hall, Ohio State's ROTC building, Captain Aubrey Whitehead, the Air Science 101 instructor, walked into the room. He was a strong man with broad shoulders and a tight-fitting shirt. He introduced himself and welcomed us to the academic portion of ROTC. "This is it," he said. "This is the last chance you have to prove yourselves to the world. No one cares how you did in middle school or high school, but everyone, for the rest of your lives, will ask how you did in college. Your GPA and your academic success here will determine your career selection upon commissioning. Your grades will stay with you forever. Remember that."

Captain Whitehead's words hit me hard, and to this day, I don't know why. His words catalyzed something inside me, a new desire to not just succeed, but to thrive, academically. I had a new mind-set, a paradigm shift. It was the first time in my life I really wanted to be successful in school. And the desire to succeed was just as strong as the fear of failure or looking bad in front of a teacher.

In high school, I had no problem missing a homework assignment or being unprepared for a class. In college, it was different. I dreaded a day where I showed up to class unprepared. I wouldn't let it happen, and in that first quarter at Ohio State, I didn't. I never missed a class from my five-course schedule: geography, math, an engineering survey class, political science, and air science. My grades were tracking high for the first time in years. I worked hard, studied at the library daily, met with professors, and went to bed at a reasonable time. I was doing my best, all anyone could ask of me, and all I could ask of myself. But I did have a problem: political science.

Despite attending every lecture and discussion class, taking rigorous notes, and reading every assignment, the themes in political science class weren't clicking in my brain. I just couldn't get it. I earned a D on one major exam and a C on another, and even though I had a good participation grade for the discussion class, it was clear I either had a C or a C– going into the final exam. A grade like that would be devastating to my overall GPA.

"Excuse me, Captain Whitehead," I said as I knocked on his office door.

"Come on in, Cadet Schaffel. What can I do for you?"

I walked in, saluted, and the captain put me at ease. "Sir, what's the average GPA for pilot selectees?"

"Probably a 3.5 or better, from what I've seen."

I thanked the captain, saluted, and departed his office. I needed a 3.5 GPA during the course of my college career. Anything like a C or a C– would be detrimental, despite having a few As. I knew I had to crush the final political science exam. Everything came down to it.

As our quarter was wrapping up, Captain Whitehead talked to our class about final exams and gave us best practices on studying and keeping a good schedule. But one piece of advice was particularly helpful. "If you want to know what's on a final exam, meet with your professor during office hours," he said. "Listen to what they have to say, then go back and study what they told you to study. Then go back again and demonstrate that you studied everything, and ask the professor again for more guidance." He paused and looked at the class. "At that point, I guarantee they'll basically tell you what's on the final exam." I decided to heed Captain Whitehead's advice.

A week before my political science final exam, I met Dr. Liddle, the political science professor, during his office hours. "Dr. Liddle, I'm having a lot of trouble in the class," I said. "I'm studying, I'm reading, and I've attended every discussion class, but things just aren't clicking for me. I'm wondering if you could give me any insight into themes on the exam, so I can ensure I'm prepared."

"Focus on the comparison between governmental systems, be able to provide examples of why one works over another, and be sure to use a good essay structure," he said. "If you can do that, I'm sure you'll do fine." I thanked him for his insight and went back to the library. I studied what Dr. Liddle recommended, and about three days later, I returned. I was taking Captain Whitehead's advice.

As I explained to Dr. Liddle what I thought were the major themes, it was clear I wasn't on the right track. His face looked puzzled, and I could tell he was getting agitated. "Parker, listen," he said. "Be able to compare a parliamentary system to a presidential system, like a country in Europe and the United States, then compare those to Indonesia's form of government, which is a mix of the two. Have a secondary focus on totalitarian regimes and any associated downfalls and benefits. Okay?"

Captain Whitehead was an oracle. Dr. Liddle basically told me what was on the exam. Any other student could have done the same thing, but I doubt any of them had. I studied what Dr. Liddle told me, focusing on the major themes he mentioned, took the final exam, and waited.

After final exam week was over, professors began to post students' grades. I was glued to my computer screen for days on end, hitting refresh on my browser like a Pavlovian dog. Then the grades started to appear.

Math – A

World Regional Geography – B+

Engineering Survey – B+

Air Science – A–

I couldn't believe what I was seeing. I hadn't earned grades like this since middle school. I knew I had done well throughout the quarter, but it was surreal. That said, everything came down to my political science grade. My entire GPA depended on it.

University policy dictated that final grades for Autumn Quarter 2002 be posted by 8 p.m. on Tuesday, December 17. That night, I was at my dad's office in Bethesda, Maryland, where he was the Chief Information Officer for a company called CoStar Group, a powerhouse in the commercial real estate information world. He was working late that night, as he usually did considering his duties as CIO, so I logged onto a computer and continued obsessively refreshing my grades page.

Click. Click. Click.

Refresh. Refresh. Refresh.

The asterisk that held the place of my political science grade remained after each reload. Until it didn't, and the asterisk changed from a star to a letter. I saw it, and I knew what it was, but it was almost like my brain couldn't comprehend what was happening. I started screaming.

"Dad! Dad! Come here!"

"DAD, IT'S A B+! I GOT A B+ IN POLITICAL SCIENCE!!!"

My dad came running over, gave me a hug, and told me he was very proud of me. He'd always wanted me to be academically successful, and now I had proved that I could do it. I realized that I must have aced the exam because there was no other way I could earn a B+ after the garbage I earned earlier in the semester. So there it was, my final GPA for my first quarter in college: 3.50.

```
        AUTUMN QUARTER 2002
OFFCRSHP&AF CUSTOM     AIR SCI    101    1   A-
ENGINEERING SURVEY     ENGINEER   100    1   B+
WRLD REGIONAL GEOG     GEOG       200    5   B+
ALGEBRA&TRIG&APPL      MATH       148    4   A
INTRO COMP POLTICS     POLIT SC   100    5   B+
     QTR: HR= 16  PT= 56.0 PH=3.50  EH= 16
DEAN'S LIST
```

A snapshot of my transcript from Ohio State showing my first quarter grades from Autumn Quarter 2002.

I even earned a spot on the Dean's List, which I later found out required a 3.5 GPA or higher. I was elated and excited, and my entire family was proud of me, especially my grandfather. I was the first of my generation of cousins to go to college, as my cousins and brother were all six or more years younger than me. My grandfather didn't let anyone forget that. "Parker has a 3.5 GPA at Ohio State," he would tell people. "He's set the standard for the other grandchildren."

Upon returning to Ohio State after winter break, I was excited to start the next term, Winter Quarter 2003. I enrolled in another math class, a tough chemistry class, a freshman English class, and Air Science 102. New classes, new excitement, and new things to learn. It was time to make it happen again.

During the second week of the quarter, I was directed to report to the office of Colonel Sheila Brocki, our ROTC detachment commander. I walked to the doorway to her office, the biggest of all the staff's spaces. It had a large L-shaped desk, pictures on the wall from her career, and military "challenge coins" seemingly everywhere. I stood at attention—my body tall, shoulders back, fingers rolled into my hands aligned along the seam of my pants, and eyes looking forward—and knocked on the door.

"Colonel Brocki, Cadet Schaffel reporting as ordered." The colonel directed me to enter and sit down. I entered the room and saluted. As I did so, I noticed that Captain Whitehead was already in the room, sitting on a chair to the left of the two-seat couch on which I sat. I was perched, my back erect and my hands in my lap, just how I had been told to sit when speaking to a colonel.

"Parker, I have some great news," she told me, calling me by my first name rather than as cadet. It seemed strange, but she was in charge. "Each year, each Air Force ROTC detachment has the authority to award a full scholarship to a new, freshman cadet without one," she said. Then she smiled. "We selected you."

I started to breathe heavily. My eyes grew wide. I looked at Captain Whitehead and again to Colonel Brocki. I began to smile, but I was stupefied. I had no idea anything like this was coming. I didn't even know this was something they did. "Thank you, ma'am," I said, managing to get out a few words. "This is fantastic news."

"It's a three-year scholarship, good for up to $15,000 per year," she said. "It will begin in Autumn Quarter 2003, next fall, the start of your sophomore year. Because you'll be on a scholarship, you'll also receive a monthly stipend, reimbursement for books, and be eligible for an academic incentive for good grades."

I was bursting with energy and trying to contain myself, but I was struggling. "Thank you, ma'am," I said to Colonel Brocki. "Thank you, sir," I said as I turned to Captain Whitehead. I saluted and left her office. I ran back to my dorm room, just a short distance away on Ohio State's south campus, and called my parents to tell them the news. They were so excited, and probably more shocked than anything else. I had graduated from high school with a 2.7 GPA, maybe a 3.0 weighted GPA, and I had just earned a 3.5 GPA in college and earned a full academic, three-year scholarship.

A few weeks later, I received a handwritten letter in the mail. It was from my dad.

Parker,

Congratulations again on the scholarship. I can't tell you how proud I am of your accomplishments. I couldn't be prouder to have you for my son. I love you very much.

Love, Dad

I still have that letter, and I always will. It felt good to have a proud father, and it was at that point in my life that he and I both recognized that I had my priorities in the right places.

A few weeks later, I was getting anxious to hear the results of my selection for a summer program. All Air Force ROTC cadets had the opportunity to apply to a variety of summer programs, paid for and sponsored by the Air Force, including programs such as combat survival training and the U.S. Air Force Academy's glider training program.

But one piqued my interest more than any other. It was called Freefall, the Academy's parachuting school, in which students complete five solo, ripcord parachute jumps and earn the U.S. military's coveted basic parachutist badge. If I made all five jumps, I could wear the badge on my uniform for life. It was the only summer program to which I applied because it was all I wanted. Captain Whitehead told us that the selection board would release their results by early April.

The quarter ended in mid-March, and I continued with my academic success, earning a 3.45 GPA for the quarter. During the one-week break between winter and spring quarter, I decided to spend my time wisely and join the Air Force ROTC unit on a trip to Eglin Air Force Base, located on a large swath of land in Florida's panhandle. The trip would give me some insight into active-duty Air Force life. Our schedule included a base tour, visits with active-duty units, and a chance to complete the base's obstacle course.

On the way back to Ohio, at some point along the 14-or-so-hour journey, I moved toward the front of the bus and sat behind one of our ROTC staff officers, Captain Bill Kossick, our chaperone for the trip. Following some small talk, I asked if he knew anything about the results of the summer program selection. "I'm not at liberty to say," he responded over his shoulder. "But I can tell you this," he added. "You *were* selected for a program, and while I can't tell you specifically which one, let's just say that you're going no farther west than Colorado Springs and that you're going to need a parachute."

I cracked a smile, thanked him, and leaned back in my seat. My smile grew wider. I thought about all the things I had earned just in my freshman year: a full scholarship, a slot in parachute training, and an offer from Ohio State to join the honors program. It was all coming together. My hard work was paying off. I was getting after it. I was making it happen. I finished my freshman year with an overall 3.41 GPA, excited to accomplish the next feat in my quest for pilot training.

I spent June and July physically preparing for my upcoming parachute training. I knew what I was in for, as I had peppered the previous year's candidate with questions before the school year closed out. Part of that preparation included intense physical training because the first thing I would have to do upon arrival to Colorado was take a physical fitness test. Any cadet who failed the test was immediately sent home. Considering the base is six thousand feet above sea level, I had to work extra hard to ensure I was ready. Day in and day out, I went to the Fitness First gym in Gaithersburg, Maryland.

Located in a small strip mall, the club's manager and staff got to know me well. After breakfast, I'd head to the gym around 10 a.m., lift weights until about 11:30 or noon, then run outside in the hot, humid, Washington, D.C.-suburb air. *The hotter and more humid, the better*, I thought. Then, I'd go to the steam room and sauna, take a shower, and be home around 2 p.m. to eat a late lunch. After two months of training, I was ready.

On Friday, August 8, 2003, I reported to the Air Force Academy, about an hour drive south of Denver. The base was as picturesque as I'd heard: a beautiful base and college campus nestled against the foot of the Rocky Mountains. It was my first time on official active duty, and what a place to do it.

I didn't sleep much that night, thanks to my anxiety and adrenaline. "Healthy nervousness," as I called it. After what felt like only a few hours of sleep, the parachute training staff picked us up at five thirty in the morning and took us from our lodging to the training area. Staff Sergeant Matt Thompson, our lead instructor, gathered us together. He didn't seem like any other Air Force sergeant I'd met before. He was about six feet tall, thin, and had a wide, infectious smile. Moreover, he was really nice.

"Welcome to Freefall!" he yelled to the 70 of us cadets, all 19-year-old kids assembled from ROTC units across the country. "Let's do some PT!" he said as he started us on a jog around the base.

After the run and some push-ups and sit-ups, we gathered around a set of pull-up bars.

"Okay, this might not make sense to some of you, but females have to do one pull-up and males have to do eight," Staff Sergeant Thompson said. "You can do more if you want, but if you can't do your minimum, I'm sorry, but we'll have to send you home." When it was my turn, I ran up to the bar and easily knocked out the eight pull-ups while another instructor watched and checked my name off his list. Every cadet passed, and shortly after we immediately started ground training.

My nameplate for my flight suit I wore during parachute training. DET 645 stands for Detachment 645, the Ohio State Air Force ROTC unit.

Thirty-six hours of ground training later, it was time to get in the plane, and then there I was, 5,000 feet above the ground, with a 100-mile-per-hour wind in my face. I jumped out and landed safely. Following two more jumps that day, and two more jumps the next day, Staff Sergeant Thompson pinned my wings on my uniform. I made it. (More details of this experience are in Chapter 2.)

When I returned to Columbus about a month later to begin my sophomore year, I had a full scholarship, a new parachutist badge, and a full head of steam. I started off the academic year with a 4.0

GPA, which earned me a $400 academic bonus from ROTC. Then I did it again in winter quarter, and again in spring quarter. I finished the year having earned straight As. Things were going as planned.

Singing the paperwork for my ROTC scholarship with then-Technical Sergeant Todd Fewell.

Taking the Oath of Office with Major Budd Zinni shortly after signing the paperwork. My mom is taking this picture.

Shaking hands with Major Zinni after receiving an award for superior performance during my sophomore year.

Although I had a fun, awesome, incredible summer program after my freshman year, the summer program after my sophomore year would be the complete opposite. Along with every other sophomore cadet, I had to attend Air Force ROTC Field Training, a five-week basic officer course that was just like basic training for enlisted service members, except that we were expected to know a lot more (we had all been in ROTC for two years) and demonstrate strong leadership skills (we were preparing to become officers).

I flew to Ellsworth Air Force Base, South Dakota, three days before my twentieth birthday. I knew what to expect because I had done my research, but no amount of preparation could prepare me for the real thing. Almost from the moment of my arrival, it was just like the movies. I got yelled at by three different officers at the same time for something I didn't even do. I slept about five hours a night and had physical training two or three times per day. Every scenario I was in had purposefully induced stress. I had to eat my entire meal in less than seven minutes, and privacy was non-existent.

My birthday came and went with no acknowledgement other than a "happy birthday" by my flight commander about six days after the fact.

I passed the time by the meals. "Two hours until lunch," I told myself. "Ninety minutes until dinner." One meal at a time. One day at a time. The days and weeks began to pass by, and I learned that keeping my mouth shut, although difficult for me, was the best way to get through unscathed. I graduated fifth out of 25 cadets in my group. That ranking was important, as it was factored into the formula for selecting future pilots. The fact that I was in the top 20% meant a lot.

Air Force ROTC Field Training – Ellsworth, AFB, Hotel Flight. I am standing fifth from the left.

Returning to Ohio for my junior year, Autumn Quarter 2004, I joined the upperclassmen and was put in charge of the oversight, training, and development of 15 freshman and sophomore cadets, the same group I was in just a year or two before. I was humbled to be offered the position, as many of my fellow cadets returning from field training vied for it, but only eight of about 30 received the position. It was a fantastic leadership opportunity, one in which I learned to lead, develop, and grow other cadets. It was something I would do on active duty with junior officers and enlisted, so I was grateful for the experience.

During the quarter, I had the opportunity I was awaiting, the one for which I had worked so hard. It was time to submit my application for pilot training selection. It all came down to a few factors on which I would be rated: my GPA, my flight ranking at field training, my physical fitness scores, my Air Force Officer Qualifying Test scores (which I took my freshman year), and my ranking in my cadet class according to Colonel Huhn, my new ROTC detachment commander who took over for Colonel Brocki after she retired. A panel of senior Air Force officers reviewed all of this information and made their selections for candidates for pilot, navigator, and air battle manager training. The process would take about four or five months, so I kept my nose to the grindstone, maintaining my high grades and peak physical fitness.

Friday, March 11, 2005 was one of the greatest days in my life. In no rush for my 9:30 a.m. history class, I slept later than I normally did. A few streams of light from the sun came through my window blinds, just enough to allow me to see my room clearly. I sat up in bed, rubbed my eyes, and grabbed my flip-style cell phone, unplugging it from the charger. The screen illuminated and displayed the time 8:33 a.m. When I opened the phone, it alerted me that I had a missed call and a voicemail. *Strange*, I thought, because I usually didn't get calls that early. When I opened the phone, I saw the missed call was from the ROTC detachment's main phone number. It could have been anything, so I checked the voicemail and heard the voice of Major Zinni. "Good morning, Parker, this is Major Zinni. I want to let you know that we received results for the aviation selection board and you were selected for pilot training. Congratulations. Please come by the detachment today to fill out paperwork."

My eyes grew wide. I inhaled deeply. Then I started to scream. "I got it! I got it!" I ran out of my bedroom across the hall to Joe's bedroom, catty-corner from mine. "Joe! Joe! I got it! PILOT TRAINING!" I didn't know if my other five roommates were sleeping, but I didn't care. This was it. It was everything for which I had worked so hard. Everything had paid off.

I immediately called my parents and grandparents to tell them the news. My grandfather responded how he always did: "Well, hey, how 'bout that. That's pretty good!" I could tell he was smiling. All my family members were excited for me. They were proud. I was proud. Although Facebook was still nascent, even for college students, I updated my status and posted the news to my friends. I returned Major Zinni's phone call, thanked him for the news, and told him I would stop by later in the day.

Skipping a shower, I put on clothes, grabbed my bag and iPod, and walked downstairs and out of my house. I walked down Neil Avenue, a small north-south street just north of the campus. I turned slightly left to head through the business campus, but to my right was Converse Hall, the ROTC building, the place I'd go in a few hours to sign my paperwork. As the music started playing on my iPod, I heard lyrics in a song that seemed to perfectly fit the moment: "We will turn it up and never down."

It was a metaphor for everything I had done since arriving at Ohio State. I was always working harder, getting better grades, and scoring higher on my physical fitness tests. For the past three years, I had been turning up my life and never turning it down. And now,

I was going to pilot training in the world's greatest air force. The future 2nd Lieutenant Parker Schaffel was only 15 months away, and pilot training was only a few months after that. Nothing was going to stop me.

After that morning's history class, I went to the ROTC building to sign my paperwork and saw about 12 other fellow cadets who were also selected to pilot, navigator, and air battle manager training, including my friend Jason Brenner. Jason was a mechanical engineer, and despite his tough major, still maintained close to a 3.5 GPA. He was shorter than me, and a bit stockier, so while he was never the fastest runner, he made up for it with his high cadet ranking, excellent academics, and a top 20% ranking at field training. It was great to know that everyone there was accomplishing their dreams. We were the future of the Air Force.

Master Sergeant Todd Fewell, our senior non-commissioned officer-in-charge at the ROTC detachment, prepared our paperwork for us. "Sergeant Fewell, good morning!" I said loudly as I walked into his office.

"Good morning, Cadet Schaffel, congratulations," he said with a bit of a country accent. Master Sergeant Fewell was from Ohio originally, but he was from the sticks, and had that twang when he spoke. He was a former Air Force Security Forces police officer, who had a Purple Heart medal for being shot and wounded in the leg while on duty. I never really knew the details but the purple and white ribbon on his uniform gave him a lot more credibility than anyone else I knew in the Air Force to that point. He had an easy, big, slightly goofy smile and was always willing to help out when I needed it.

"Okay, I need you to read this over, and when you're ready, initial here, and then sign at the bottom." I read through the document, outlining my selection to pilot training and my commitment to the Air Force if I completed pilot training: 10 years. I initialed and signed.

"Congratulations, again," Master Sergeant Fewell said. I thanked him, shook his hand, and went to Buffalo Wild Wings near campus to celebrate with the other cadets. Granted, I was still three months short of being 21, but felt I had a worthy cause to have a drink.

During the next ROTC-wide function the following week, those of us selected for aircrew training stood in front of the entire detachment and Colonel Huhn pinned our cadet pilot wings on us. The wings were entirely symbolic, as they only signified being selected for pilot training. Still, I now had two sets of wings, the cadet pilot wings and my basic parachutist badge. There was only one other cadet in the detachment who had both, so I was in a unique crew, and I could sense the underclassmen's admiration.

A picture of the nameplate I wore on my flight suit after receiving selection to pilot training.

I finished winter quarter with another 3.83 GPA, took a week off for spring break, and hit it hard again for the spring quarter, during which I was selected for another ROTC summer program called Operation Air Force. The program placed cadets between their junior and senior years in an operational Air Force unit for three weeks so they could experience active duty and get a good sense of what the particular occupation is like.

Because of my selection to pilot training, I was assigned to the 77th Fighter Squadron, "The Gamblers," at Shaw Air Force Base in South Carolina. The 77th was one of the three squadrons of the Air Force's 20th Fighter Wing, and all three squadrons flew the F-16 Fighting Falcon, or what F-16 pilots called the Viper. My sponsor, an Air Force major and F-16 pilot whose call sign was Rider, called me a few weeks in advance of my trip to give me some insight into how the three weeks would unfold. "You'll basically be a part of our squadron," he told me. "You'll see what it's like to live a pilot's life, and hopefully we can get you up in the air."

In the air? In an F-16? Me? I couldn't wait. The time until the start of my assignment couldn't come fast enough. When I flew to Columbia, South Carolina, in mid-July 2005, Rider picked me up and drove me the 45 minutes back to the base, dropping me off at my billeting. It was a small, one-bathroom efficiency, but it would do for three weeks.

The next morning, I reported to a mandatory breakfast with Air Force officers and cadets from other ROTC units and the Air Force Academy. After some brief introductions, we were dismissed to our units. I went to the 77th Squadron headquarters, and Rider showed me around.

"Come here after your daily breakfast meeting, and we'll see if we can get you in operational planning meetings, so you can see what flight planning is like," he said. Rider showed me the gear room, where all the pilots kept their flight gear. He showed me the weather squadron, where Air Force meteorologists provided weather updates to the squadron. And, of course, he showed me the bar.

"This is where we come on Fridays after we fly," he said as he opened the swinging door. It was incredible and reminded me of something out of *Top Gun*. The bar itself, a horseshoe shape, loaded with all different kinds of booze (but a lot of whiskey), lined the left side of the room. About 30 beer mugs hung from the top of the bar, and each had a pilot's call sign, a picture of an F-16, and Air Force pilot wings. Across the room were several tables and a popcorn maker. I had turned 21 just a few weeks before this, so I was hoping to be able to imbibe with the rest of the squadron when the time called.

"I've got to handle some other responsibilities," Rider said. "But feel free to walk around and introduce yourself to everyone when you see them. They all know you're here, so we want to get you integrated fast." I thanked him and wandered around the squadron, introducing myself to everyone I could. At the end of the first day, I went back to the bar, empty at that time, and looked out the windows to the flight line. F-16s were lined up in perfect formation on the taxiway. It was a beautiful sight, one I would never forget.

About a week and a half later, one of the other pilots, call sign Smash, told me that the 77th Squadron was soon getting its rotation of the F-16 D-model, the two-seater F-16. Most F-16 models are one-seater planes, except the F-16D, which has two seats and is used for training purposes. The base only had one of these models, and the three F-16 squadrons shared it on a rotating basis. "Squadron leadership wants you to fly," Smash told me. "Just make sure you get all the prerequisites done so you're cleared to rock and roll when the time comes."

Smash was talking about egress training, in which you practice disengaging yourself from a plane on the ground, a checkup with a flight surgeon, and altitude chamber training. Altitude chambers, located on most Air Force bases, were small rooms that could become depressurized to simulate oxygen levels at altitudes up to about 30,000 feet and gave aircrew the experience of what it is like to become hypoxic, a deficiency in the amount of oxygen in the human body. While I had already completed egress training, I contacted the altitude chamber on the base and asked for a slot in the next training.

"I'm sorry, Cadet Schaffel," the sergeant told me. "It's currently down for repairs and will be back up in about a week and a half." I didn't have a week and a half. I had only two days until I was supposed to fly. I wasn't going to miss my chance. A 2nd lieutenant assigned to the squadron, whose call sign was Dredge, helped me schedule a slot in altitude chamber training for the next day at Langley Air Force Base in Virginia Beach, Virginia. I just had to get there. The base was about a six-hour drive. I contacted the rental car agency on my base and rented, with my own money, a vehicle to make the drive to Virginia. I arrived at about eight o'clock that night, grabbed a quick bite, and headed to bed. My training started the next morning.

As the only cadet out of the five of us in the course, I joined two other lieutenant colonels, a major, and a captain for the training, which consisted of some briefings and eventually our time in the chamber. I donned my mask, which was just like the mask in an F-16, and began to run through the protocols, including answering questions on a sheet of paper.

The altitude level indicator, in bright red LED lights, started to go up. Five thousand. Ten thousand. Fifteen thousand. "Okay," a voice said over the loudspeaker. "This is the usual altitude at which humans can maintain normal oxygen levels. We will continue our ascent shortly." The numbers continued to climb. Twenty thousand. Twenty-five thousand.

"Participants," the voice said. "Please breathe regularly for six seconds, then complete your forms." I could tell I was getting woozy, my eyes struggled to focus, and I was starting to giggle to myself.

"Are you angry?" one question asked. "What is 2 + 3 x 3 + 2 x 3?" asked another. The point of the questions was not to pass or fail, but to help aircrew recognize when they *are* hypoxic, so they can take corrective action, either by fixing an air leak in the cockpit or descending to an altitude where they will get more oxygen. After the training, I received a completion certificate, and immediately drove back to South Carolina. I arrived around ten o'clock at night and would be flying in an F-16 in less than 12 hours.

The next morning, after breakfast, I walked to the squadron and reported to the operations room. Dredge walked me back to the gear room to get me suited up for the flight, including a helmet, mask, harness, and a G-suit, which was designed to prevent blackouts caused by blood pooling in the lower part of the body during acceleration in a fast turn.

The two patches from the 77th Fighter Squadron. The patch on the left was worn Monday through Thursday, while the patch on the right was worn on Fridays. While assigned to the squadron, I wore these patches on the shoulder of my flight suit.

Ready to fly, I waited in the bar until the squadron's operations chief, a lieutenant colonel whose call sign was Chemo, told me it was time. Chemo didn't have cancer, nor did he ever have it, as I found out, but when he discovered he was going bald he decided to shave his entire head, hence his call sign. Chemo and I, along with three other pilots, walked out to the flight line and up to our planes, parked in the same place I saw them on my first day in the squadron. The crew chief, an Air Force staff sergeant, saluted Chemo, and placed the ladder next to the cockpit. Chemo climbed in to the front seat, threw his gear bag into the seat behind, and started to strap himself in.

"Sir, you'll love this," the crew chief told me as he placed the ladder next to the back seat.

"Thanks, sergeant. It's my first time, and I hope it's not my last." I climbed up and slid into the cockpit, carefully lowering myself into the seat, grabbing Chemo's gear bag.

"Parker, just jam that thing behind your seat. If we have to eject, we won't need it anyway!" Oh, boy. If we have to eject? I was hoping I didn't vomit all over the cockpit. My nerves were running high enough as it was, and then the pilot made an ejection joke 10 seconds after I sat down.

The cockpit was one of the most incredible things I'd ever seen. Buttons everywhere. Gauges. Meters. Control panels. Yep, just like the movies. I strapped myself in, just as I learned in the egress training, connected my G-suit to the port in the dash, and pulled out a clear plastic bag, placing it under one of the elastic straps on the right leg of my G-suit. While pilots usually used these elastic straps to secure mission plans and flight routes, I put the bag there in case I needed to barf.

"Nine out of 10 people flying in a fighter for the first time vomit," the flight surgeon told me before I got in the plane. "It's okay if you do, but you gotta make sure you barf in the bag or you'll be cleaning the cockpit yourself."

After systems checks and a near cancellation of the mission because of a technical glitch, we received clearance to take off, and closed the cockpit. Chemo started the engine, and we received clearance to proceed to the taxiway. Just like in the movies, the crew chief came to attention and saluted as we went by. Chemo returned the sergeant's salute and steered the plane to the end of the runway as we waited for the other three planes to join.

"You okay back there, Parker?" Chemo asked me.

"Yes, sir. Doing great. Really excited for this."

All four planes aligned. Chemo shot the throttle forward, engaging the plane's afterburner. My body pressed back into the seat. I could feel the force of our acceleration on my chest. We lifted off and quickly gained altitude. In what seemed like no time, we were in the air headed to a training range. As we made our way, we flew in the finger-four flying formation, comprising a lead element and a second element, two aircraft of each. When viewing the formation from above, the positions of the planes resemble the tips of the four fingers of a human right hand (without the thumb), giving the formation its name. As I looked, I noticed we were the second element leader, the ring finger.

About 15 minutes later, we arrived at the training range, and Chemo and the other pilots started aerial maneuvers. "Let's see what you can handle, Parker," Chemo said on the radio. He banked the plane on a 45-degree angle and pulled back on the joystick, turning us sharply. I felt the G-suit start to fill with air, adding pressure to my legs to keep the blood flow restricted. The more G-force on the plane, the more air is pumped into the suit, helping lock down blood flow in a pilot's legs. Chemo banked us again, now the other way, and with each turn, I noticed the G-suit adding more pressure to my legs and the G-meter getting higher.

3.7, 4.5, 5.2 . . .

"You okay, Parker?"

"Yes, sir! Loving every minute of it!" And I was. I was nervous, and I was scared, but I was loving it. In that moment, I recognized how incredible it is to experience something so few people do. I felt more energized than ever to know that I would get to do this *for a living* in a little more than a year. After a few more air maneuvers, some of which were done by hand signal between the pilots, Chemo came back on the radio. "Parker, you ready to fly?"

"Yes, sir!"

"Okay, ready?" I slowly gripped the joystick with my right hand and throttle with my left hand.

"You have the controls," Chemo said, using the standard language between two pilots to recognize who is in overall command of the plane.

I gave the standard response: "I have the controls."

"Parker, the plane is yours. Let's keep the throttle where it is, but why don't you go ahead and test out the joystick? Remember the plane is fly-by-wire, so it's sensitive, but try it out."

This was everything I dreamed of. I was a 21-year-old Air Force ROTC cadet, flying an F-16 fighter plane at close to 700 miles per hour over the open skies of South Carolina. It was *actually* happening, and I was so happy, so thrilled, to be there. And the fact that I would get to do this for a career made it that much sweeter. After about 30 seconds, Chemo took back the controls to continue conducting maneuvers with the other pilots.

"Parker, you ready to rock and roll?"

"Yes, sir!" I said, although I had no idea what he meant. The next thing I knew, the plane banked 90 degrees to the left, and we were flying sideways. Chemo pulled back on the joystick and brought us into an extremely tight left-hand turn. The G-meter start to spike.

6.0, 7.0, 7.5, 7.8.

The G-suit tightened, I controlled my breathing, and tensed my muscles as hard as I could, doing everything in my power to maintain the oxygen flow to my body until we pulled out of the turn.

"Damn it! I wanted eight Gs that time!" Chemo shouted into the microphone. Chemo banked us to the other side and again pulled back on the stick. I repeated my techniques, locking my muscles and breathing in short bursts while I tried to gain some cognizance of what we were doing in the air.

"Yes! That's what I'm talking about. 8.1 Gs on that one!" Once more, he rolled us back, and we hit 8.2 Gs. Chemo was kicking my ass. I felt nauseous, and I wanted to throw up, but I hadn't yet and I was doing everything in my power to keep it that way.

After a few more maneuvers, we reformed our finger-four flying formation, made our way back to the base, and landed the plane, pulling into the same spot from which we took off. Chemo cut off the power to the engine and opened the cockpit. I removed my mask, disconnected the G-suit, and grabbed our gear bags from behind the seat. Chemo turned around and shook my hand.

"Great flight, and great job," he said.

"Thank you, sir, that was absolutely incredible." I almost forgot about the plastic bag, still tucked in the elastic strap of my G-suit. It was dry. I hadn't touched it. I was the one in 10. The crew chief brought up the ladder, and we hopped down to the tarmac. Chemo turned and gave me a high-five.

As we walked back from the flight line to the squadron head-quarters building, we were joined by the other three pilots from our flight group. One of them, a rotund major whose call sign was Joker, walked over to us. "Hey, Chemo, how'd he do?"

"I kicked his ass up there, but he hung in for every bit," Chemo said without hesitation.

While I kept my bearings and maintained a normal facial expression, on the inside, I was elated. I felt, in that moment, as if I had been accepted into the fighter pilot community. I wasn't a pilot, but I felt like I belonged. I had performed my rite of passage. As we walked up the sidewalk to the squadron headquarters, I was hum-bled and grateful for the amazing experience I just had. I thought about how excited I was to get back to school, graduate, commission, and join the real ranks. One day, I'd fly one of these on my own.

I had no idea at the time, but that F-16 would be the last plane I would ever fly.

A few weeks after I returned from South Carolina, the Air Force ordered me to Brooks Air Force Base in San Antonio, Texas, to complete a two-day physical, as part of the process to become medi-cally cleared to be a pilot. The testing was more invasive than any test I had undergone before, but I understood the circumstances as the Air Force was considering putting me in control of a $100,000,000 aircraft. I was administered every test imaginable: echocardiogram, eye dilation, urinalysis, blood work, measurements, and a hands-on physical with a physician. At the end of the second day, my final task was to meet with a doctor to talk about my medical history. "Do you take any prescriptions?" he asked.

"Yes, sir," I said, as I reached into my pocket, pulling out a small tube of cream. "I take this medication called Elidel, which I use for some dry skin on my nose."

I didn't think it was a big deal. I wanted to be honest and follow the first value of the Air Force—Integrity First. As long as I was honest, everything would be fine, as there was nothing wrong with me.

"Hmm, this isn't pre-approved for air crew," he said. "But don't worry, I can get you a waiver. I've gotten waivers for this before, so it shouldn't be a problem." His assurance was good enough for me, and following the physical, my colleagues and I returned to Columbus and awaited the start of our senior year.

By the start of Autumn Quarter 2005, all of my fellow cadets had received their medical clearance letters. I had not. "I'm worried about your status," said Master Sergeant Todd Fewell. "Delays like this aren't good. And it's not just your flight status I'm worried about. It's your commission." Master Sergeant Fewell was experienced, and he knew his stuff. It was clear he wasn't joking.

The next day, Thursday, October 13, Master Sergeant Fewell called and told me that he received a letter from Air Force Medical Command regarding my physical. I was at the ROTC building as part of my normal Thursday schedule, so I stopped in his office to see him and read the letter.

"Cadet Schaffel must obtain a private consultation regarding his use of the prescription medication Elidel," the letter read. Discouraged but obeying the order, I called a local dermatologist and scheduled an appointment for the next day.

The next morning, I drove to the dermatologist's office located in Gahanna, a northeastern suburb of Columbus. The receptionist sent me back to a dark room located in the back of the office, where I sat on an examination table and waited for the doctor. A few minutes later, he knocked and walked in.

"Good morning," he said as he looked down at a folder he was holding. "Parker. Hello, and happy Friday! What brings you in today?"

"Good morning, doctor. I'm a cadet in Air Force ROTC at Ohio State, and I've been selected for pilot training."

"Congratulations!" he interjected. "That's exciting!"

"Yes, it is, but as part of my flight physical, they have requested I see a doctor about this," I said as I handed him my tube of Elidel cream. "I was diagnosed with dermatitis when I was younger, and my dermatologist in Maryland prescribed Elidel to control it. I've used it ever since and don't have any problems." I was being honest. If I used it, my condition wasn't even noticeable. The worst I would ever have was a few flakes, just like having dandruff.

He looked closely at my face. "Yeah, I can see that, but you probably don't need to use Elidel. You can probably use something over-the-counter, and it should work just the same." I thanked the doctor and asked him to write a letter summarizing my visit, so I could send it to the Air Force Medical Command. "Sure thing," he said. "I'll even sugarcoat it, so it sounds better."

I drove back to the ROTC building and gave a copy of the letter to Master Sergeant Fewell, who told me that, after he submitted it, the Air Force Medical Command had 45 days to review the document and provide a final response. I went home and spent the rest of the day pondering what would happen.

The officers at the Medical Command didn't take 45 days to reach their decision. They took seven.

Thursday, October 20, 2005, was one of the worst days of my life. As I got ready for the day, I donned my Air Force service dress uniform, which included a long-sleeved button-down shirt, tie, and jacket, as was required by the order of the day. I was proud of it. I had earned more than 14 different ROTC ribbons, including special, unique awards from the American Veterans and the War of 1812 Society, physical fitness ribbons, honor and merit ribbons, and more. I wore a blue and yellow aiguillette, an ornamental braided cord, representing my membership in Air Force ROTC's Arnold Air Society, an ROTC subgroup that promoted Air Force values, culture, and history. But most importantly, atop my ribbon rack, I had the two badges of which I was most proud: the basic parachutist badge and the cadet pilot badge.

I stood outside my bedroom door, looking at myself in a long mirror that hung across the wall, admiring my uniform. Knowing the decision on my fate could come at any day, I decided that, if this was going to be my last time wearing it, at least I'd go out looking good.

At about two thirty in the afternoon, as all my fellow cadets were in our weekly Leadership Laboratory class, I was directed to report to Colonel Huhn's office. I knocked on his door, entered the room, saluted, and sat on the same small couch on which I sat when Colonel Brocki told me that I was awarded the three-year academic scholarship. The colonel sat behind the wooden desk. To my left was Major Rod Caraway, an ROTC staff officer and Air Science instructor for senior cadets. He was sitting in the same spot in which Captain Whitehead sat a few years before. Sitting next to me on the right side of the two-seat couch was Master Sergeant Fewell, the man who helped me sign my scholarship and contract paperwork.

"Cadet Schaffel, I am sorry to say this," Colonel Huhn said. "But the Air Force has decided, because of your skin condition, to medically disqualify you from Air Force ROTC and honorably discharge you." He paused. "You will no longer, from this point on, attend Leadership Laboratory or physical training. You can choose to remain in Major Caraway's Air Science class at your discretion."

My eyes widened. My vision blurred. My body rocked back and forth. Others in the room might have been speaking, but I didn't hear it. I looked down at the floor and choked back my tears, struggling to keep my emotions inside. But I couldn't much longer. I wanted to burst. I started to breathe heavily, on the verge of hyperventilation. I stood up and looked down at Major Caraway. His elbows were on his knees with his head in his hands. I turned and gave the colonel a passing gaze. As I walked out of the office, I saw Master Sergeant Fewell's face. He was crying, and it seemed as if tears had been coming down his cheeks for some time. He cried, I think, because he respected me.

I walked out of the colonel's office, moving quickly through the lobby of our detachment headquarters to the stairwell. As I pushed the door open to the stairs, two of my best friends and fellow cadets from ROTC, Andrew Galusha and Jason Brenner, were about to walk inside.

"Hey, man, what happened?" Andrew asked me.

I could eke out only a few words. "It's not good."

I ran down the stairs and out of the ROTC building, crossed the street, and collapsed on the first bench I could find. I bawled uncontrollably, and I kept crying until I had nothing left. Everything fell apart a mere 50 feet from the same spot where I celebrated my pilot training selection. In a handful of words from a colonel and a hasty decision by an Air Force doctor, I lost everything for which I had worked so hard. Everything was gone. My life's dream was shattered. No pilot training. No commission. No Air Force. Nothing.

From the bench, I called my parents to tell them the news. I could barely make out the words as I began to cry again. "The Air Force is discharging me," I told them through my broken, cracked voice. They knew this was possible, as I had told them the news the previous week.

"Oh my, I'm so sorry, Parker," my mom told me. "I know how hard you worked for this. I just can't believe it." I couldn't believe it either.

The hardest phone call to make, however, was the call I made to my grandfather, the one whose footsteps I wanted to follow, the one who was going to commission me into the Air Force in a matter of months, and the one who had already brought a new Air Force uniform to wear to my commissioning, as retired officers were allowed to do. We were both going to be on the same stage, at the same time, with both of our hands in the air, repeating the same lines of the same oath that he swore when he commissioned in 1953.

I dialed. He answered. "Hi, Grandpa." Those were the only words I could get out before I started crying again.

"Parker, are you okay?" the 72-year-old man asked me.

"No, Grandpa, I'm not okay. The Air Force . . . " I began to stutter. "The Air Force is . . . discharging me." I began to cry again. "Because I have dry skin."

He was silent, and I kept crying. I don't remember what he eventually said as my wails were too loud to hear his response. "I'm sorry, Grandpa," I said as I hung up the phone.

After the call, I stumbled back to my apartment and upstairs to my room. I positioned myself in front of the same mirror in which I had admired my uniform just hours before. My intuition had been right. This was the last time I would ever wear the uniform. I stood there and began to cry again, tears streaming down my face as I looked at my wings and ribbons. All my accomplishments, aligned perfectly on the left breast of my blue jacket, seemed to mean nothing in that moment. I unbuttoned the jacket and took off the Air Force uniform for the last time.

Neither my appeal to the Air Force Medical Command nor my letter to Senator Warner from Virginia, a member of the Senate Armed Services Committee, changed my fate. I received my discharge a few weeks later.

After I grieved and regained my footing, I considered my options. What was I going to do now? It was late November, and I was still on track to graduate in June, so I only had a few months to determine what to do after that. I was no bum. I was the guy who got after it. I had to make something happen.

My desire to serve in the military for the United States was still strong, so I took Colonel Huhn's offer to help me find a place in another ROTC unit on campus. He introduced me to the Army ROTC battalion commander, an Army lieutenant colonel, who told me that he thought I would be a great fit in the Army program. I had outstanding physical fitness and a 3.7 grade point average.

"And that stuff about a face cream," he said. "Don't even worry about it. You'll be just fine here." I agreed to join and enrolled in the next quarter's Army ROTC class, Military Science 402.

Initially, I was excited to join the program. I'd still have the chance to commission in the military, and maybe my grandfather would be able to commission me after all. Maybe I could be a helicopter pilot, or an intelligence officer, or something else. I didn't know, but I wanted to see what could happen. Unfortunately, my time in the Army would be short-lived. After joining, the Army seemed disinterested in any of my preferences, telling me that I would go to the career path in which they wanted me and that I would have to attend double the training of anyone else because I transferred into the program. The final straw was the accusation by an Army ROTC cadet that I had been harassing a junior cadet. Accusations like that were serious, so I contacted the university's staff to launch an investigation. They found that the accusation was fabricated because the cadet who reported me didn't like me and thought I hadn't paid enough "dues" to join the Army ROTC program.

"If this is the way the Army works, I don't want any part of it," I told my mom. I wrote my intention to be discharged in a letter to the lieutenant colonel. He accepted my resignation without comment, and, because I had signed a contract just a few weeks before this, I received another discharge from the U.S. military, my second in six months.

Then it was April, and I had two months to figure out what to do after college. "Parker, you've had a lot of ups and downs this year," my mom told me. "It's okay to move home and figure things out." Moving home, to me, was not an option. I was a guy who got after it. I turned it up but never down. In an attempt to land *something,* I attended a university-sponsored career fair, featuring mostly sales positions. I was grateful that my good grades and interpersonal skills landed me an interview and eventually a job offer to be a financial adviser with Ameriprise Financial, a financial planning and services company.

I moved to Westlake, Ohio, a nice suburb on the west side of Cleveland, and was very successful in my new job. But despite my success, my desire to serve the United States in one capacity or another never wavered. In Westlake, I was serving my clients and myself, but I needed something more. The service I truly wanted to give was to my country. I was grateful to live in the United States and wanted to use that patriotism in my work, so I looked up jobs in the United States Intelligence Community and applied to be a military analyst at the Central Intelligence Agency. I made it through the clearance process and began working at the CIA the following summer. While it wasn't a military commission, I felt that I was at least serving my country. It was the best I could do. (For the lessons I learned as a financial adviser and my decision to change jobs, read Chapter 3.)

If luck is action in the face of opportunity, then I got lucky a few months into the job. As I was having a friendly chat with two of the analytic managers in my office in December 2007, I found out that one of them was a captain in the Navy Reserve. "That's really cool," I told him. "I was close to commissioning, but it didn't happen."

"What do you mean?" he inquired. I explained my story and told him that I was at least in a better place because I was working in intelligence as a civilian, if not in the military. "If you're still interested in commissioning, you should check out the Navy's direct commission program," he said. "It's a quick way to get in the door, and you'd have a good shot because they want intel officers."

I thanked him for the information and told him I'd consider it. I debated internally if applying was even worth it. The Air Force said my skin condition was a disqualifier, but I found out later that I could have gotten a waiver if the Air Force wasn't looking to make cuts from the ranks because it had too many people. The Army didn't care about my issue, but that didn't work out for other reasons. In the end, I decided I would try out the Navy, as it required nothing more than effort to research the process and put together an application package.

That night, I researched the direct commission program and found that it was a pretty genius idea. The program took civilians with strong leadership attributes and applicable work experience in certain Navy-related fields—like intelligence, engineering, and public affairs—and commissioned without any further special training. I had the leadership training, thanks to my experience in ROTC, and I was now working as an intelligence analyst, so I had the real-world experience, albeit not a lot. I decided to apply.

The next day, I contacted Lieutenant Commander Joe Phillips, the local Navy officer recruiter, and stated my interest in the program. After a few introductory emails, he directed me to schedule the Aviation Selection Test Battery, the Navy's equivalent of the Air Force Officer Qualifying Test, which I took my freshman year of Air Force ROTC. The main difference was that the Navy's test had a section called "officer aptitude rating."

"That's the most important score," Lieutenant Commander Phillips told me. "You need a minimum of 35. If you don't get that, we can't even consider you." I took the test a few weeks later in January 2008 and earned a 57. Now qualified to apply to the program, I completed the rest of the application package and sat for an interview with four Navy captains who asked me about my experience in intelligence and my leadership attributes, as well as how I would react in various scenarios. Following the interview, the recruiter sent my application package to a selection board, which would determine my fate. It was my third and probably final attempt to commission in the military.

Another few weeks went by, and I received the email from Lieutenant Commander Phillips for which I was waiting: "Parker, the Intel results have been posted. You were not selected, HOWEVER, your package was 'tabled,' which means it will be reviewed at the next Intel selection board (date TBD). We should not have to update anything prior to that next board, but if we do, we'll let you know."

Ugh. It wasn't a no, but it wasn't a yes. It was a "we'll see." The next day, his assistant, Chief Petty Officer Rhonda Denton, called and told me that the applicants whose applications were tabled would go to a special board in a few weeks, and I would be reviewed then.

Then I received another email.

"I misspoke yesterday by saying the INTEL 'tabled' applications would go to board on May 1st. The current information available from the command is that the next board is still to be determined."

Back in purgatory, I thought. Another waiting game.

In June, I learned that the next selection board planned to convene in October, and I hoped they wouldn't need anything extra from me in the meantime because I was heading to Afghanistan for a short work stint and might not have access to certain documents they might request. (For more information on my time in Afghanistan, read Chapter 4.) While I was in Afghanistan, Lieutenant Commander Phillips changed assignments, and I received an introductory email from his replacement, Lieutenant Brian Harper, who told me he had all the information he needed for the board. With a sigh of relief, again, I waited.

I returned from Afghanistan on Monday, October 20, 2008, three years to the day since I found out the Air Force planned to discharge me. The day still burned me deeply, but returning home from a war zone on the same day gave it a slightly better taste. Two days later, I was back on the Ohio State campus, assisting the CIA's Recruitment Center with an information session for students interested in intelligence. While walking across the Oval, the large grass- and sidewalk-filled plot of land in the middle of campus, my phone rang. It was Lieutenant Harper. "Parker, I have some good news for you."

"Yes, sir." I stopped walking and listened.

"I wanted to be the first to congratulate you. The results from the board are in, and you were selected to commission into intel."

"Yes! I got it! I got it!" I started to scream, uttering the same words I did when I was selected for pilot training. I cared little for the scene I was making in the middle of campus. This was my moment. I raised both of my arms, looked to the sky, and screamed again, eventually bringing the phone back to my ear. "Sorry, sir. I'm just very excited. Thank you. This is great news!"

"We'll be in touch on next steps. Congratulations, again."

I called my parents and told them the news, and they were thrilled, but just as before, the most important phone call I would make was the one to my grandfather.

"Grandpa, three years and three days ago, I called and told you that you were not going to be able to commission me," I said. "But today, I'm happy to say that you *will* be able to commission me. The Navy just called and said I was selected to commission in the reserves."

"Hey, well how 'bout that," he said. "That's pretty good!" It was the same response he gave me when I was selected for pilot training. I could tell me was smiling. "Harriet!" I heard him yell to my grandmother. "Parker is going to get into the Navy!" I smiled. Nothing was official yet, but this moment was mine.

The next step in the process was the one I dreaded most: a two-part physical, including a review of my medical history, urinalysis, and blood work. In the first appointment, the nurse handed me the medical history form, a standard form all of the military branches use. Have you ever had cancer? No. Diabetes? No. Epilepsy? No. Heart disease? No. Skin condition? No. I made the conscious decision to be less than honest. I decided that, at that moment, my skin was fine, so I didn't have any "condition."

I learned through my experience with the Air Force that honesty was not integrity and vice versa. Honesty got me discharged and my dream taken away. I wasn't going to let it happen again. I was going to do the right thing and give myself a chance. I had a lot to offer the military and was going to give myself the opportunity to serve. If they found out about it, so be it, but I decided I wasn't going to be forthcoming. The only question to which I circled "yes" was the question that asked if I had ever been discharged from the U.S. military. Then, I waited for the response.

January and February came and went with no news. Then came March. I was still hopeful, but getting more nervous by the day. I emailed Lieutenant Harper: "Sir, I heard from some other selectees via an online message board that some good news came in for them today. Is there anything about which you can inform me?"

"Parker, do you by chance have a copy of your exit physical from the Air Force?" he responded via email about an hour later. "It seems the Navy wants to see it."

Here we go again. I could see it all happening before my eyes. Another military branch, another failed attempt. The events of that terrible day in October 2005 replayed in my head.

I didn't exactly have an "exit physical," although I still had the paperwork the Air Force gave me about its reasons for discharging me. But I didn't want to incriminate myself, so I made the decision to withhold the information and told Lieutenant Harper I didn't have an exit physical. I wasn't lying, but I wasn't being completely forthcoming.

"Okay, it shouldn't be a problem," he said. "The only thing I think I'll need is your DD-214," he said, referring to the standard discharge paperwork for U.S. military service members.

"I'm sorry, sir. I was only in ROTC, so I didn't qualify for one when I was discharged."

Another month went by with no updates from Lieutenant Harper, so I emailed him again. He responded quickly: "I'm trying to get an answer about your Air Force physical. Do you have some kind of skin condition?"

Again, the scab that never seemed to heal. Dry skin was coming back to haunt me, but I had learned my lesson and decided, again, that plausible deniability was my best option. In that moment when I received the question, my skin was clear, albeit a hint of red, but I wasn't scaly, had no rashes, flakes, or anything else. As far as I was concerned, there was nothing wrong with me *at that exact time.* "Sir, I do not."

The following month, the Navy Medical Command sent Lieutenant Harper a directive for me to see a doctor to obtain a diagnosis of my "skin condition," just like the Air Force had done four years before. The directive wasn't a denial of my commission, it just asked for more information, and more information is what I would get them. This time, however, things would be different. I knew the mistakes I had made in 2005, and I was not going to repeat them.

Per the order, I scheduled a physical with a doctor, but not a dermatologist. The physician specialized in internal medicine, and I chose him because, although I had never seen him before, I knew of him through several family members and therefore he knew about me.

"Good morning, Parker," the doctor said as he walked in the exam room. He was a squirrely-looking man who seemed to be in his sixties. We shook hands. "What brings you in today? Your paperwork says something about a military physical."

"Yes, doc, I'm applying to join the Navy, and they asked me to obtain an assessment from a doctor on two things: an assessment of my physical readiness for military service and a determination as to whether I have any skin lesions of any kind."

"Skin lesions?" he said, looking puzzled.

"Yeah, I'm not sure," I said. "That's what the paperwork from the Navy said."

"Strange request, but okay, I'll give it a look." He laid me down on his exam table, performed reflex checks, and checked my eyes, ears, and mouth. After about five minutes, he sat me up again. "You seem fine to me, and I don't see any skin lesions."

"Thank you, doctor. Could you please put that in a letter for me so I can send it to the Navy?" He nodded.

A few days later I received the letter, which I sent to Lieutenant Harper for forwarding to the Navy Medical Command. In mid-June, I received the response from the Navy, eerily similar to the letter I received from the Air Force four years before. I was disqualified from military service due to dermatitis.

Again?! I couldn't believe it. A doctor verified there was nothing wrong with me. What was the point of going to him if his letter didn't matter? At the bottom of the Navy's letter, I saw a glimmer of hope. "Medical Command will reconsider its decision if it receives a copy of the applicant's DD-214 and a letter from the applicant indicating any current medications." I had been through this before and knew this was a possibility. It was time to make my last-ditch effort to save my chance at commission. That evening, I wrote my rebuttal letter and asked for a reconsideration of the decision, based on four criteria:

The doctor's determination that I was in excellent physical condition and had no skin lesions of any kind

My certification that I did not take any medications

Information I included from a University of Arizona medical study that indicated dermatitis tends to disappear as people reach adulthood, which I compared to a letter I attached from the Air Force that recommended me for military service if my condition was nonexistent

An explanation for why I did not have a DD-214, the military discharge paperwork

Again, I was being less than honest. I wasn't taking any prescriptions at that exact moment, so I felt like that was good enough, and stated as such. I printed out the letter and provided copies of the medical study, the Air Force paperwork, and the letter from the doctor and mailed them to the Medical Command.

The remaining days in June ticked by as I anxiously awaited a response. On most days, I went to work at seven thirty in the morning, checked my personal email and mobile phone voicemail repeatedly, and left saddened at four in the afternoon, knowing that if I hadn't heard from Lieutenant Harper by then, I wasn't going to hear anything that day. I would arrive at my home about 30 minutes later and ride my bike for an hour or two on a local bike trail. I'd ride for miles, thinking and hoping that I would get some good news and that all my hard work would eventually pay off.

A few weeks later, on the morning of Tuesday, June 30, I emailed Lieutenant Harper and asked for a status update. He responded a few hours later and told me that he didn't know anything but that he'd send something as soon as he did. I departed work at four, as usual, and drove home. I didn't have a smartphone, so I couldn't check email in my car, so when I got home I immediately pulled open my laptop to check if I had any correspondence from Lieutenant Harper before he left his office for the day. I had another message from him. It must have come in when I was commuting home. I clicked on it, and saw that it contained no text, only an attachment. I opened it and started reading.

"Based on a review of available medical information, subject applicant DOES NOT meet established physical standards due to chronic atopic dermatitis, chronic seborrheic dermatitis."

Ugh. Here we go again. Same story, different day. I kept reading.

"A waiver of the physical standards IS DISAPPROVED for Unrestricted Line."

Waiver is disapproved. I couldn't win. There was more to the letter, so I kept reading.

"A waiver of the physical standards IS APPROVED for Restricted Line/Staff Corps only. The waiver code to be assigned is HCB."

Wait.

Waiver.

Approved.

Restricted Line.

Intelligence officers were part of the Restricted Line.

I was approved!

I did it!

I made it! I got it!

Eight years, three military branches, two discharges, two contracts, and more emotional ups and downs than I ever could have imagined, and I finally got what I wanted. I was approved for a commission in the U.S. Navy Reserve. My emotions shot through the roof. I was beaming with excitement, jubilation, and energy. I jumped around my living room.

I needed to do something with the energy. I had to celebrate. I went for a run outside on a local trail, stopping at a clearing in the woods. I stood there, looked around. No one was there. It was just me, so I screamed—as loud as I could—and I kept screaming. Eight years of pent-up happiness, anger, sadness, disappointment, and trepidation all came out at once. I continued yelling until I fell to the ground and began to cry. A moment I will never forget.

It was real. It was actually happening. I did it. I would be able to accomplish my dream. I never gave up. I never stopped. I never quit. I got after it and made it happen.

August 11, 2009, was one of the greatest days of my life. A beautiful summer morning, the air still cool from the night before as I drove to Andrews Air Force Base, located just southeast of Washington, D.C. in Maryland, about a 45-minute drive from my home in Virginia. My grandparents, parents, and brother met me there, outside the Navy Reserve building.

I was wearing the Navy summer white uniform: a white, short-sleeve shirt, white pants, white shoes, and a white cap. I hugged my family, and we walked into Lieutenant Harper's office together. My parents watched over my shoulder as I signed the paperwork for my eight-year commitment, just like they had done six years before when I signed the contract to join the Air Force with Master Sergeant Fewell.

Putting the last few signatures on paper, moments before the Oath of Office.

With the paperwork complete, we walked outside toward the flight line and stood in front of a flagpole. On my uniform above my left breast pocket, a piece of metal glistened in the sunlight. It was my basic parachutist badge, the one badge no one could ever take away. On the far side of the runway, I noticed several F-16s parked and lining the taxiway, just as I remembered them from my first day at Shaw Air Force Base in 2005. I looked at my badge and looked at the planes. I smiled. I stood in front of the flagpole, and across from me stood my hero, my grandfather, Major Arthur Sturm, U.S. Air Force (Retired). He had a smile on his face. I knew he was proud. He raised his right hand and asked me to raise mine. My family watched. I knew they were proud. My grandfather spoke, and I repeated:

I, Parker Jeffrey Schaffel,

Having been appointed an Ensign in the United States Navy Reserve,

Do solemnly swear to support and defend

The Constitution of the United States

Against all enemies, foreign and domestic,

And that I bear true faith and allegiance to the same,

And that I take this obligation freely,

Without any mental reservation or purpose of evasion,

And that I will well and faithfully

Discharge the duties of the office upon which I am about to enter.

So help me God.

Taking the Oath of Office with my grandfather, a picture which still makes me shed tears of joy every time I see it.

Immediately upon completing the Oath of Office, I hugged my grandfather. It was a hug I'd waited to give for eight years.

This story was one of the most impactful of my life and the reason I listed it first in this book. I learned many lessons along the way to reaching this goal that I still consider today.

Integrity is not honesty. When prompted by the doctor to reveal the medications I was taking, I lived by the Air Force core values: integrity first, service before self, and excellence in all we do. *Integrity first*, I thought to myself. *Do the right thing, tell the doctor about my condition and medication, and everything will be okay.* Except it wasn't okay. My actions led to my discharge. Years later, I realized there was a difference between integrity and honesty; they were not one in the same. Most parents lie to their children about things like Santa Claus, the Easter Bunny, and the Tooth Fairy, but we don't fault them for that. They're being dishonest, but at the same time, I argue that the decision is one of integrity—doing the right thing by keeping their children's imaginations alive.

I put this lesson to the test when applying to the Navy. It was clear that the Navy would not have let me commission if I had admitted to having, or if a doctor had confirmed, any sort of skin condition.

In the end, I served honorably for eight years in the Reserves, trained dozens of sailors in intelligence analysis, and deployed overseas to the Middle East, an assignment in which I was awarded the Joint Service Achievement Medal and the Navy Accommodation Medal. Withholding that information led me to serve with integrity in the world's finest navy.

You can wish you did something differently without regretting the decision you made. To this day, I wish I would have kept my mouth shut to that Air Force doctor during my flight physical. If I had, he wouldn't have known anything, I would have commissioned in the Air Force on June 11, 2006, the day of my graduation, along with all my friends, standing on stage with my grandfather. I would have gone to pilot training shortly after and probably would have become a pilot, serving a 10-plus-year career in the Air Force. I'd probably still be flying today. But I also could be dead.

I was 29 years old on April 3, 2013, when I read a report that an F-16 crashed shortly after taking off from Bagram Air Base in Afghanistan. The pilot, Captain James Steel, was also 29 years old, and was stationed at Shaw Air Force Base, assigned to the 77th Fighter Squadron. He was my age, flew the same plane I wanted to fly, and was assigned to the same squadron at the same base to which I was assigned back in 2005. I could have been in that same plane on that same day. I now have the perspective to no longer regret my decision about telling the Air Force about my condition, because if I had done so, I might have been in that plane on that day. At the same time, I wish I could have had the chance to fly.

Value your intuition; it's there for a reason. After the first week of excitement of being in the Army ROTC program, wearing Army uniforms, and learning new Army things, I had a gut feeling that something wasn't right. As the weeks went on, and the Army

ROTC commander retracted many of the promises made to me in the beginning, I started to question my decision. I didn't want to make a hasty decision on my future in the Army simply on gut instinct, so I flew home and discussed the situation with my family and assessed the entire situation with the counsel of those I most trusted. I told them what had been happening, discussed the pros and cons of staying in the program, and asked their advice and opinions on the options I had. Only once I assessed the facts and compared them to my instinct did I make the decision to leave the program. Trust your intuition for what it is, but ensure you gather all the facts you can and weigh them equally with your intuition before making a final call.

Some decisions you take lightly may have significant, unintended consequences later. During this eight-year endeavor, I made several quick decisions that had far more strategic consequences for me, both positive and negative, than I ever imagined they would:

Choosing history as my major: I chose to study history because the Air Force said I could pick any major I wanted for my scholarship. I could have been an engineer, a chemist, or anything else, but I decided I wanted to study something in which I knew I would do well academically and for which I had a natural passion. My goal, after all, was to go to pilot training and I needed a top-notch GPA for that—the subject of my degree would not matter. While studying history limited my options in the private sector, succeeding in my studies opened the door for me to work as a military analyst at the CIA, and working there started the process of me commissioning in the Navy.

Choosing to live in the suburbs of Cleveland rather than stay in Columbus: I'll never forget the conversation with Ameriprise manager Marc Miller when he asked if I wanted to work in Columbus or Cleveland. "Wherever I'll do better," I told him. This was a critical decision that I took far too lightly. Living in the Cleveland area, however, led me to realize that I was unhappy there, which increased my motivation to leave. I applied to the CIA, received an offer, and those events led to meeting the Navy Reserve captain.

Never give up, never stop, and never quit, unless you *really* don't want it anymore. It took me eight years and three branches to commission in the military. "Most would have given up after the first attempt," one of the editors on this book wrote to me. But I didn't. I didn't because I had a dream to serve as an officer in the military. I had a dream to serve my country, and I wasn't going to let anything stop me as long as I felt there was another way. If the Navy didn't let me in, perhaps I would have tried the Marines. If that didn't work, I'd be out of options and maybe, at that point, I would have given up, and that would have been okay. It's human nature to lose motivation for goals, and that's perfectly fine, but as long as you have a goal, don't let anything or anyone stop you.

I served in the Navy Reserve from 2009 to 2017, receiving an honorable discharge following eight years of successful service. I separated from the Navy having earned the Intelligence Dominance Warfare Badge, the Joint Service Achievement Medal, Navy Achievement Medal, Overseas Service Ribbon, Global War on Terrorism Expeditionary Medal, Global War on Terrorism CONUS Medal, National Defense Medal, Expert Rifleman Medal, and the Expert Pistol Medal.

CHAPTER 2

GAINING CONFIDENCE: HOW A MOVIE, A FOOTBALL COACH, AND A SKYDIVE CHANGED ME

"Dude, what are you doing tomorrow?" my friend Bob asked me on the phone one mid-August day in 1999. It was a few weeks before the start of my sophomore year of high school.

"Nothin'. What's up?"

"You should play football with me and Rich this year. Equipment pickup is tomorrow. You should come."

"I don't know, man, you really think I should?"

"Just be there," he said as he hung up the phone. I thought about it for a while. I had played defenseman on a hockey team for years, so I liked to bodycheck opponents. In football, I could tackle opponents, so maybe Bob was on to something.

"Hey, mom, I think I want to play football this year. Bob told me signups and equipment pickup is tomorrow. Would you mind taking me?" I asked her that night.

"Sure. Doing nothing after school for the fall is not an option, so I'm glad you found this." My mom knew that I needed to stay busy and that coming home after school would probably just lead to me playing computer games or being unproductive. Football would ensure I had more structure in the fall.

The next afternoon, she drove me to the high school gym where the varsity and junior varsity coaches were signing up players and handing out equipment. I saw Bob in the check-in line.

"This is it, man. You ready?" he said as he put his hands on my shoulders and started to lightly shake me.

"I don't know, dude. We'll see how tomorrow goes," I said with a slight smile. I was excited, but I was nervous. I'd never played football before, and I had no idea what to expect, other than the rumors I heard that, when two-a-day practices started, you entered the equivalent of hell for two weeks.

When Bob and I were issued helmets, I tried mine on but couldn't see a thing. My hair, which was about cheek-length, covered my eyes. "Might have to do somethin' about that hair, son," one of the assistant coaches told me. I took off the helmet, received the rest of my gear, and stored it in the already smelly locker room.

"Mom, I think I need a haircut," I said as I opened the car door. "I tried on my helmet, but I couldn't see a thing." The next thing I knew I was sitting in a chair in a small barbershop near our house.

"Come on in, son," the barber said as he motioned to his chair. "Am I using a one or a two?" he asked as he secured the cape around my neck.

"How do you know I want you to buzz it that short?"

"I've had plenty of you football players come in and tell me that you need your hair chopped off because you start practice tomorrow." He was right.

"I guess I'll go with a two." Without hesitation, he turned on the clippers and ran them over my head several times. Long locks of highlighted, slightly green hair fell to the floor. I had dyed it earlier that summer with a friend. In less than two minutes, my hair was gone. I looked at myself in the mirror and felt my scalp, noticing the prickly yet interesting feeling of having hair that short. There was no turning back now.

The next day, the first day of two and a half weeks of two-a-day football practices, was unlike anything I had experienced before. Each practice was three hours long, twice as long as any hockey practice I'd ever had. The entire junior varsity (JV) and varsity football teams would show up around 8:30 a.m., and the other JV players and I grabbed our pads and headed to the field to start practice at nine.

"Not a second late!" Coach Thompson, our head JV football coach would yell. "If a single player is one second late, y'all are gonna run!" I didn't see what the big deal was. We were going to run anyway. And then we were going to run some more. That was how two-a-day practices went . . . for two and a half weeks until school started. The morning practice was dedicated to physical conditioning: sprint drills, strength training, and agility work. The afternoon practice focused on the game: offense, defense, and special teams. Practices were held Monday through Saturday. The only day off was Sunday.

It was insanely difficult, but every day got just a bit easier, and one day in particular would be the day when I left my mark on Coach Thompson and the rest of the team. After a brief water break, in which we drank from a hose connected to a multi-holed PVC pipe, Coach Thompson called us back to the field. "Thirty seconds! Let's go!"

"Hats on, boys!" I yelled, encouraging my teammates to put their helmets back on. "And on the hop!" I said as I started jogging back to the field.

"I like that motivation, Parker," Coach Thompson said to me. "So, you're first up for the next drill." I nodded. He looked at our team. "You boys ready?!"

"Yes, sir!" We all shouted in unison.

"I really mean it! YOU BOYS READY?"

A roar deafened.

"Good! It's time for 'Hit it'!" The premise of the drill was simple. One kid took a football and tried to run between two cones, about five feet apart, while another kid stood between the two cones and tried to stop the ball carrier. It was the drill that radiated respect. It was all about who could hit the hardest.

I went up against a kid named Dave. We came from the same grade, were equally sized, and both were new to football. Coach Thompson handed me the ball. Dave stood on the line between the cones, as Coach Thompson started barking orders. "Ready! Don't let 'em cross that line!" he yelled at Dave.

"You better get through those cones!" he yelled at me. The whistle blew. I put my shoulder down and ran right at Dave. Our pads crunched as our bodies struggled against one another, until I spun and crossed the line.

"Do it again!" the coached yelled. The whistle sounded. I tried to dive for one of the sides, but Dave tackled me outside of the cone.

"Again!" Another whistle. With a head of steam, I charged at Dave and struck his facemask with my right forearm, giving his head a blow, and knocking him down and onto his back. I walked over him across the line.

"Yes!" Coach Thompson screamed. "I like my starting strong safeties to be able to hit!"

Starting strong safety? Me? A week later, in our first scrimmage, Coach Thompson put me at the top of the depth chart on defense. I was the strong safety. But there was one problem. I wasn't confident. I wanted to make a good play, but I was nervous about making a mistake. I wanted to win, but I didn't want to get hurt. These dichotomies played in my mind as the games went on, and the coaches noticed my hesitation. I lost my starting position after three games, and I never got it back.

The next year, the summer between my sophomore and junior years, I went through two-a-days as I had done before, but by the end of the trial, I decided I wasn't interested in going back to practice. The seniors were bigger, stronger, and faster than me, and I wasn't having fun anymore. "What are you going to do instead?" my mom asked. "Doing nothing is not an option."

Later that night, my mom took me to see *The Replacements*, a movie that had just come out in theatres about a week or two before. It featured Keanu Reeves and Gene Hackman and told the story of replacement players for a professional league, which was facing a strike by its regular players. It told the story of a quarterback, played by Reeves, who lost his self-confidence. Reeves's coach, played by Hackman, led him through the struggle of regaining his confidence, enabling him to make the plays and eventually win the important game at the end of the movie. I felt like I was watching a version of my own story on screen. After the movie was over, we walked out of the theatre, and turned to my mom. "I think I'm going back to practice tomorrow."

"Good. I'm glad to hear that, because doing nothing is not an option," she said as she smiled. I had no idea at the time that my decision to go back to practice would ultimately lead to a series of events that would change my life and my entire mind-set. I would eventually learn what confidence was and how important having the right confidence at the right time truly is.

While I didn't play much my junior year, I returned to play my senior year. It was probably my last opportunity to play organized tackle football in my life. Before our senior season, our team got a new coach, Doug Miller. He was a former member of the University of Maryland Terrapins football team in the mid-1980s, and he brought with him a new staff of experienced assistant coaches. It was a new opportunity to demonstrate that I deserved to be a starter and that I could make the plays when it mattered. I worked hard and continued to get better, stronger, and faster.

"Listen up!" Coach Miller barked the day before our first scrimmage. "Depth charts for offense and defense are posted on the locker room. Special teams will be discussed later. If you're at the top, you earned it. If you're number two or three, you better work your ass off to get to number one." After he dismissed us, we bolted to the locker room door to see the chart. I found my name. Starting outside linebacker on the defense's right side. Bob was to my right, playing middle linebacker.

"Yo, B!" I yelled to Bob. "First team, dude!" We high-fived and celebrated with the other starters on defense. I had never played line-backer before, always defensive back, but I was willing to give it a shot. It was a new coach, a new season, a new year.

"Your job is simple," Coach Miller would tell me. "Don't let the running back get outside of you. Contain him inside. If there is a pass, cover the flats."

In our first game, I was matched against a kid on the other team's offense who was about my size. Equally matched, I felt confi-dent. In our next game, I was in a similar situation, matched against a tight end who was about my size, maybe a bit bigger. I felt like I held my own. The game went down to the wire, and we lost by a touchdown. Despite the loss, I was proud, not only of my team, but of myself.

The next week, however, everything changed. On a humid night, my team and I walked out of the locker room onto the football field of Northwest High School, a powerhouse football program in our division. During our pregame warmups, I looked across the field to the other players. They were gigantic. They were fast. They were mean. They'd look back at us and taunt us. "Come on, white boys! Y'all ain't got nothin' on us! Bring it!"

I, on the other hand, was terrified, and it showed. I got man-handled by Northwest's tight end, who was easily 50 pounds heavier than me. I didn't, and felt like I couldn't, accomplish my primary responsibility—keeping the run contained—and Northwest's running back swept around the outside of our defense multiple times in the first half, gobbling up yards. At halftime, Coach Miller spoke to us in the locker room. "What the hell is going on out there? Jesus Christ, Parker, how many times did you get hooked on sweeps?"

"Three, sir." Our team lost the game by more than 30 points. It was a crushing defeat. When watching the game film the next morning, the entire team watched me as I got hooked by Northwest's tight end again and again and again. I felt like a failure. Our team was certainly outmatched, but nobody else had the egregious errors I did. Entering the next week of practice, I wasn't sure of my status: would I still be a starter on defense? Would the coach kick me off the team for playing so badly?

As we started practice on Monday afternoon, I was still part of the first-team defense. But the next day, Tuesday, was a day that would change my life forever. An exchange happened that I'll never forget. Our defense was practicing different formations against an offensive group that was simulating our next opponent, Richard Montgomery High School. I was playing outside linebacker and was going up against one of our tight ends. The quarterback hiked the ball and handed it off to the running back, who started running toward my outside shoulder. The tight end tried to hook me, but I kept my outside shoulder free and stayed outside of his reach, moving down the line of scrimmage and forcing the running back inside.

"DO IT AGAIN!" Coach Miller screamed.

The offense ran the play again. Again, I contained the run to the inside. "THAT'S IT! I'M NOT DOING IT ANYMORE!"

We all looked at Coach Miller, having no idea what he meant, until he pointed directly at me. "Parker, I've had it! I'm not playing you in games anymore! Every week you come out here and show that you can do it in practice, but you get in the games and you choke! You're a practice player, and I'm not gonna have it anymore!" He threw down his clipboard and stomped off to talk to the other assistant coaches.

I stood there, utterly stunned. My teammates stared at me. I felt worthless. I had just been called a practice player in front of the entire team. I had just been called out for being a failure. Coach Miller stuck to his word, too. I didn't play in the game the following week, and in the game against our biggest rival, I played only three downs, replacing a briefly injured teammate.

Following a difficult conversation between my dad and Coach Miller, I eventually switched positions from linebacker to safety, the position I had played during my sophomore and junior years. I eventually regained a spot on the first-team defense more so because I was the best option around rather than Coach Miller's confidence in my abilities. I made some great plays in the final games, but I received no lesson, no memory, that was more visceral as that late-September afternoon on the practice field when I was called out for not being able to perform when it mattered. I was called out for being a practice player. It was a lesson I would never forget, and one that would shape the course of my life.

These are the only two photos I have of myself playing football. In the first picture, I'm standing on the right side of the picture, waiting for the opposing team to hike the ball. In the second picture, I'm on the ground having just made a tackle.

Two summers later, in early August 2003, I flew to Colorado Springs, Colorado, to attend the U.S. Air Force Academy's Freefall program, the summer training for which I had been selected during my freshman year in ROTC at Ohio State. It was a very exclusive program, as each Air Force ROTC unit in the country only had one slot. My ROTC commander picked me, and I joined about 70 other cadets to jump out of perfectly good airplanes. Five jumps total. Solo freefalls with 10-second delays. No static line to open my parachute for me. No instructor to do it for me. It was all on my own.

After passing the mandatory physical fitness test on the first day, we broke into training groups of about 10 cadets each, led by a member of the official Air Force Parachute Team, the team that performed in skydiving competitions and special events across the country. Our flight lead was an Air Force major, a short, blond woman who had logged thousands of skydives. It was rare for an officer to be on the parachute team—they were mostly enlisted—and I felt grateful to have such a qualified instructor.

This was the patch worn by the training staff of the 98th Flying Training Squadron. I traded my Ohio State AFROTC Det 645 patch for this with one of the staff members.

Our group walked into a massive hangar with a vaulted ceiling that was easily 30 feet high. Rows of training harnesses and helmets lined one side, while mockups of the U.S. Air Force UV-18B "Twin

Otter" aircraft, the plane we would jump out of, lined the other side. Padded, blue safety mats covered the floor. Five-foot-wide large placards, enlargements of the 98th Flying Training Squadron's seal were mounted on the opposite wall. "This is where you will spend the next 30-plus hours of ground training," our instructor told us. "Now let's get to work."

Our training, as I found out, was broken down into buckets, exiting the plane, body positioning, in-air movements, under-canopy movements, and landing on the ground (what instructors called a parachute landing fall or PLF). "Each training module is built on the previous one," the major said. "You must progress as a group, so each of you needs to help out your fellow cadets when necessary."

During our first break, I started talking with another cadet in my group, Ryan Sanfilippo. He was in the Air Force ROTC program at the University of Washington but grew up in Colorado Springs. He was an inch or two shorter than me, had blond, cropped hair, and blue eyes. He reminded me of myself, just from the complete opposite side of the country.

Throughout the first day, Ryan and I became battle buddies, a term used in the military to describe a close friend who helps you stay on the right track and keeps you out of trouble. Ryan seemed motivated, prepared, and most importantly, confident. He knew his stuff coming into the program and had done the same research I had done before the course even began.

"Everybody on the ground," the major commanded. "On your bellies. We're going to learn the proper body position during your jump. Watch me." I dropped down to the blue, padded floor and copied our instructor. I brought my arms off the ground and bent them at 90-degree angles. I lifted my legs, so the toes of my boots hovered about eight inches above the floor. "I want you flexible but firm. I should be able to rock you like a saucer. The only thing touching the ground should be your hips."

I felt like we had been in the position for five minutes, holding it. "Deeper. Arch harder!" I pushed myself to the max, arching my body as hard as it would go. "Okay, drop it." We took a short break. "Back up! Arch!"

After what seemed like a few hours practicing how to arch our bodies, we moved to the mock-up of the plane to practice exiting. I was already sore, and now we had to simulate arching our bodies after "jumping" out of the door of the plane. "Listen up!" the staff sergeant called out. "This is going to be one of the most important parts of your jump. If you don't exit the plane correctly, your whole jump could be screwed, so pay attention."

The instructor, a slightly stocky guy with brown hair and sideburns as low as possible but still within regulations, stepped into the door, which was about four feet wide by four feet high. "When you jump, one of us instructors will be inside the plane, holding onto your harness while you get in position like this." He started to get into position.

"Right hand inside the fuselage and left hand outside, like you're holding a book between two hands. Then bring your right foot up to where the floor of the plane meets the fuselage, and make sure your toes are a little outside the plane. Bring your left foot behind your right, bring your right knee outside the fuselage, and push your hips forward."

I envisioned what that looked like, and it seemed like I was going to be basically hanging out of the plane. Was that right? Was he serious?

"It's going to feel like you're basically hanging out of the plane." I was right. He was serious. "The reason you want your hips forward," he said, "is to ensure that you are able to arch your body, which is critical to having a successful jump."

He paused for a moment and looked at us. "The second really important part of this is the check-out process. You've got to get this language right to ensure that we know when to release you. If you screw it up, bad things happen."

"The check-out process goes like this. You say 'check in,' and the instructor will respond with 'check out.' At that point, look at the propeller and yell 'prop,' raise your body slightly and yell 'up,' bend your knees and yell 'down,' then yell 'arch' as you leave the plane, pushing your hips forward as far as they can go while bringing your hands down behind your hips."

That was also important, the staff sergeant told us, because having our hands down by our hips to start was necessary for our bodies to level out. "The relative wind coming sideways across the plane is going to hit your body. If you bring your arms up, you'll flip, if you keep your arms down and bring them up slowly, you'll level out, and that's what we want to see."

He ran through the whole sequence, and each of us followed, citing the proper verbiage referred to as "boldface." In the military, boldface verbiage were commands or actions that had to be memorized, forward, backward, inside, and out, under any and all circumstances. It was used in every branch of the military and a lot in combat operations. If you recited it incorrectly or couldn't recite it at all, you almost certainly failed the training class.

After the first day, I was sore, and so was Ryan. "How you feeling, dude?" I asked him.

"Man, my back hurts already, and I hit my right knee on the mock-up. I think it's bruised."

I felt the same way. After dinner, which we ate at the Air Force Academy's dining hall, we headed back to our rooms and tried to relax for the evening.

The next morning started the same as the day before: physical training, a light breakfast, and then it was straight back to the training hangar. We built on the lessons from the day before, incorporating the training into even more complex situations. We were strapped in harnesses, raised off the ground, and ordered to simulate the entire jump sequence. I watched Ryan first and grabbed my one-use camera to grab some pictures of him mid-training. When it was my turn, I felt like I was ready.

A staff member jerks the harness suspending Ryan's body above the ground as Ryan goes through his pull sequence.

Strapped in the harness and raised about four feet off the ground, one of the two instructors barked the first order. "Stand in the door!" I simulated standing in the door with my knees aligned and hands together.

"Check in!" I yelled.

"Check out!"

"Prop! Up! Down! Arch!" I yelled as I pushed my hips forward and arched my body. I brought my hands down beside my legs and began to count off using the boldface language. "Arch thousand! Two thousand! Three thousand! Four thousand!" My elbows were now at 90-degree angles. The instructors were jerking my body left and right to simulate the feel of dynamic wind resistance.

"Five thousand! Six thousand! Arch thousand!" I arched my body further as the instructors kept tugging on my harness. "Look thousand!" I yelled looking at my simulated rip cord, shifting my arms to maintain balance and grabbing the handle. "Pull thousand!" I yelled as I punched out the rip cord from the strap. "Check thousand!" I looked up at my non-existent canopy, imagining what it would be like if I had a 300-square-foot canopy above my head, filled with air, as I float 3,000 feet above the ground.

But the instructors didn't let me have that moment. The moment I initiated the post-opening boldface and said the first line of "check canopy, shape, spin, and speed," one of the instructors jumped in.

"You've got a bag lock! Your parachute won't open!" he yelled. "Take an action!" Earlier in the day I learned that a bag lock, which is when the canopy fails to leave the bag it's stuffed in, is one of four situations in which I would cut away my main parachute and deploy my reserve.

"Bag lock!" I yelled. "Arch! Look! Grab! Look! Pull! Grab! Pull!" I pulled my cutaway and reserve parachute handles, again "releasing" a canopy that didn't exist. "Check canopy, shape, spin, speed."

"All looks good," the other instructor said. "You have a rectangular canopy, flying straight, and are cruising at a normal speed." I initiated the rest of the boldface sequence, including looking around for other jumpers, turning off my reserve automatic activation device, releasing and checking my brakes, and orienting myself to the drop zone. "Good job, Schaffel, come on down."

We finished the day with several hours of parachute landing falls, a specific maneuver that helps parachutists land on the ground properly without injuring themselves. We started from one foot off the ground and eventually worked our way up to six-foot-high plat-forms, jumping into a padded surface.

"You think that's what it's going to be like?" I asked Ryan at the end of the day.

He was as unsure as I was. "I don't know, man, I still can't believe we're going to be jumping out of a plane tomorrow." I couldn't believe it either. While I had the same training everyone else had, and therefore was clearly prepared and motivated, I was nervous. I was scared.

The mood in our rooms that night was subdued. Every cadet's mind was focused on the next day, which would start at 5:00 a.m. I didn't get much sleep that night, and I'm sure others didn't either. It was still mostly dark when we arrived at the hangar, as the first rays of light were peeking out of the horizon and dancing on the mountain range to our west. We hopped out of the vans and walked into the hangar to hear the plan of the day.

"Good morning!" Staff Sergeant Thompson said with a grin. He was always happy, with a wide smile, even at the earliest hours of the morning. "Everyone ready to skydive today?" We all cheered and clapped. "Okay, this is how it's going to work. Each team will make their jump with their respective instructor. After that, we'll send you back up in the next available plane, depending if you need retraining or are set to go immediately. Good luck today and remember to trust the training!"

My 10-person team was jumping third, and because we were one of the first three teams, we had the chance to gear up first. Ryan and I, along with the rest of our team and instructor, walked into the gear room, where we were outfitted with parachutes, helmets, goggles, and altimeters. Several civilians, who worked at the unit as parachute packers and other assistants, helped us don the gear.

I stepped in front of the blue harness and rig and turned so my back faced the parachute. "Step in here first," one of the women said as she held the right leg strap. "You can't get the thing on right if you don't do the legs first." She started to laugh. I chuckled, mostly out of nervousness. "Okay, pull it up."

I grabbed the harness, put my arms through the shoulder straps, and pulled the leg straps up to my groin. I first secured and tightened the chest strap, the most important piece of the system. If it wasn't secured properly, I'd fall right out of the whole thing, 3,000 feet until I went splat. "Looks good," she said, looking at the chest strap. "Now tighten the leg straps and you'll be set."

There I was, standing in a line with nine other cadets, carrying a 300-square-foot main parachute, and a 200-square foot reserve parachute on my back. I had a large altimeter mounted on my chest strap, a blue helmet on my head, and a pair of goggles on my eyes. I was wearing an Air Force flight suit and black leather boots. *Fitting,* I thought, *as I am about to fly through the air myself.* I looked down the line at Ryan. He winked. I gave a thumbs-up.

"I need everyone to look at the board across from you and answer each question with 'yes' or 'no,'" the major said. She called out the questions one by one: "Have you had any alcohol in the last 12 hours? Have you had adequate crew rest? Have you had the opportunity for eight hours of uninterrupted sleep? Are you feeling sick?"

No. Yes. Yes. No. Then came the final question.

"Are you ready to do this?"

"Yes, ma'am!" we all yelled in unison.

"Follow me." The major walked to my right to the front of our line and opened the door to lead us out. By this time, the sun had come up over the horizon, and we could see clearly. It was a beautiful day, the air was crisp and cool, and there wasn't a cloud in the sky. It seemed like a perfect day to jump out of a perfectly good airplane, not that I knew any different.

As our line turned to the runway, I could finally see the airplane, the engines of which I had heard spinning as we left the equipment room. There it was, the UV-18B Twin Otter aircraft, one of only two owned by the Air Force. It was a great skydiving plane, our instructors told us. Its wings were mounted at the top of the fuselage, which gave a cleaner exit. It had a large jump door and turbo-propellers to get us up to altitude quickly.

Our instructor hooked up a ladder to the open door, the same door we'd be jumping out of in just a few minutes. She gave each of us a fist bump as we climbed the ladder and entered the plane, which had two rows of seats for the 10 of us plus her. The first cadet in would be the last out; the last in would be the first out. Luckily for me, I was right in the middle, giving me just enough time to mentally prepare but not dwell on the seriousness of the endeavor I was about to undertake.

We buckled our seatbelts and gave the cadet in front of us an equipment check. I stuck out my thumb, indicating the cadet in front of me was good to go. Ryan was jumping in the second pass, the one right before mine. We bumped fists once more as the plane began to taxi. As it turned at the end of the runway, the engines roared and we accelerated quickly.

Everything became a blur as I started to run through all of my boldface verbiage in my head. Prop, up, down, arch. Check canopy, shape, spin, speed. As we passed 1,500 feet, we disengaged our seat-belts, and my mind started to race. I looked out the window and lost all perspective of reality. I couldn't tell if we were 2,000 or 15,000 feet. We were *way* up in the air. We leveled off at 5,000 feet above the ground. The sound of the engines changed to a hum, and the red light next to the jump door illuminated. We were close, but not there yet.

The jumpmaster threw open the jump door, held onto the inside of the plane with one hand, and leaned into the void, looking to see when we were directly over the drop zone. She wore her U.S. Air Force Parachute Team parachute with a deep-blue skydiving suit and a cool-looking helmet. She would complete her jump after all of us.

She motioned for the first two jumpers to move to the back of the plane. The pilot switched the light from red to green. Time to fly. One after another, each cadet checked in, and in no time, they were gone. About two minutes later, we made another pass at the drop zone for the next two jumpers, Ryan included, then he was gone. Then, it was my turn. Our instructor motioned for me to move to the back of the plane where she gave my equipment one last check. She looked out the jump door, and the light switched from red to green.

"Stand in the door!" she yelled.

I placed my right hand inside the fuselage and my left hand on the outside. My feet in place, I pushed my hips forward. I turned back to the major, who was holding the right side of my harness. The hurricane-force winds were in my face and blowing the left side of my body. "Check in!" I yelled back to her.

She nodded. "Check out!"

"Prop!" I focused my gaze on the propeller. "Up!" I inched slightly taller. "Down!" I bent my knees and pushed my hips forward. "Arch!" The instructor let go as I left the plane. "Arch thousand!" I yelled aloud though no one was around to hear me now as I was plummeting to the earth. "Two thousand!" I continued to fall as I felt my body start to turn to the right. "Three thousand!" I said as I realized my eyes were closed. I opened them. In that instant, I saw I was falling through the air and that there was nothing between me and the ground. And also in that instant, I lost count. What number was I on? Oh, no! The training kicked in.

"If you lose count, start your pull sequence," the instructors beat into our brains.

"Arch thousand!" I deepened my body's arch. "Look thousand," I said as I shifted my gaze to my rip cord and transitioned my hands to maintain my stability, my left hand by my head and my right hand grabbing the rip cord. "Pull thousand!" I shouted as I punched out the rip cord, releasing the pin that kept the pilot chute contained. In that moment, the spring-loaded pilot chute flew out of the harness, caught air, and pulled the bag, in which the canopy was folded, out and into the air. "Check thousand!" I yelled as I looked up and saw wind fill the canopy.

It was big and beautiful, filled with air. "Check canopy, shape, spin, and speed." All looked good to me. I had a large, rectangular canopy, I was flying straight, and at a good speed. Just how it was supposed to be.

"Look around for other jumpers," I said, scanning the sky for the other cadet who jumped on this pass. "Check altitude. Turn off reserve automatic activation device." I was a bit above 3,000 feet, and, for the first time, took a look at my surroundings. It was breathtaking. I could see the peaks of the Rocky Mountains and the sun rising in the east. I could see downtown Colorado Springs and its buildings, some of which were glimmering in the morning light.

"Release brakes, check straight flight." I pulled down the brakes and released them, increasing my speed just slightly. "Check right," as I looked to my right. "Right 90." I made my turn. "Check left. Left 90." Same thing to the other side. "Full stall," I said as I pulled down both brakes, simulating stalling the canopy and landing on the ground. I ended the boldface with the final step: "Orient myself to the drop zone."

At around 1,000 feet, I entered the right-hand landing pattern, as was briefed to us by the instructors. At this altitude, I needed to be at the southwest corner of the drop zone. By 600 feet, I was at the northwest corner. After two more slight turns, now down to about 400 feet, I flew straight, both arms up, heading straight for the middle of the drop zone. As I got closer to the ground, I pulled down on both brakes, attempting to stall the canopy.

Wait! I was too high up. I was farther away from the ground than I thought. The training kicked in. "If you stall too high, keep your arms down, lift your wrists slightly, and perform a parachute landing fall." I lifted my wrists and performed the fall from about 10 feet off the ground. My toes hit the ground first, but I fell forward onto my right knee, rather than to the side of my body as I was supposed to do. My knee immediately hurt, but it wasn't excruciating. And because I didn't want to give any indication, I stood right up and began to collect my canopy.

After walking my gear back to the hangar, I joined the rest of the cadets, some of whom were talking about their first jumps, and those who hadn't yet jumped but wanted all information possible.

After a quick chat, our instructor pulled us into the video room to review our videos. The training squadron filmed each of our jumps with a telescopic video camera, so they could watch and rate each of our jumps on a three-point scale. A score of three was passing, two was marginal (but still a pass), and a one was rated as a failure. A jumper could get a rating of one for being unsafe in the air—things like pulling the rip cord too soon or too late, pulling the rip cord while upside down, or a number of other things.

We all sat down and watched the videos of each jumper, one by one. When it came to me, I saw my body leave the plane. My arms were down by my sides, as they should have been, but I was kicking repeatedly, a natural response to try to level out my body. The problem was that this was an unnatural experience, and kicking did nothing when falling at terminal velocity toward earth. I kicked for a few seconds, eventually became still for a second, then pulled my rip cord, releasing the large canopy above my head. My skydive lasted about six seconds, so I was within the 5-to-10-second range for a good jump. I stayed belly to earth and pulled the rip cord in the proper body position.

"Nice jump, Parker," my instructor told me. "I'm rating you a three with no retraining required." We worked through the rest of the jump videos, and our instructor dismissed us based on our groups. "Threes go back to the scheduling room to get slotted for the next jump. Twos come with me for a discussion before you suit up again. Ones will need retraining before you get back in the plane. Remember, one more failure and you're out of the program."

Out of the program for two failures. They gave you one chance to improve and that was it. I felt bad for the group who got ones, but it happened, and that's why this was training.

Before I knew it, I was geared up and back in the plane again. But this time was different. This time I actually had the self-awareness to realize what I was doing. I WAS ABOUT TO JUMP OUT OF A PLANE!

Seriously? I was doing this? The first jump it didn't really hit me. I was in such a haze and so focused that I didn't really know what was going on. But this time was different. I knew exactly what was happening. I knew what standing in the door meant, and all that came after. I started to get nervous, really nervous. My jumpmaster, a male Air Force major with short, dark hair, called for me to come forward.

I heard, "Stand in the door!" as it was my time to jump. I skirted toward the back of the plane and took my place in the door. Hands, feet, knees, and staring at the propeller. "Check in!"

"Check out!"

"Prop! Up! Down! Arch thousand!" I left the plane. Six seconds later I pulled my rip cord and released my parachute. As it opened, my body twisted, putting me into a spin as the canopy filled with air. The lines between my harness and the canopy were twisted and wrapped around each other. My training kicked in. Bicycle kicks!

I bicycled my legs, generating a spin in my lower body. Slowly, but surely, I began to spin out of the twisted lines. A few seconds later, I was under a rectangular canopy, flying straight at a good speed. I continued my checks and oriented myself to the landing zone. Jump two was complete, and I received another three rating. "Nice jump.

But next time, open your eyes," he said as he laughed. I didn't even know I had closed my eyes.

The day was starting to get later, as the sun was making its way toward the mountains to the west. We couldn't jump at night. It was unsafe for new jumpers. Most parachutists wait until 50 or 100 jumps to make their first night jump.

"We've got enough time for two more jump groups," one of the instructors said. I would be in the second to last group. My third jump of the day. I was already tired and, although I didn't realize it at the time, had expended most, if not all, of my adrenaline on the first two jumps. When it was my turn to jump, I stood in the door, placing the fuselage between my hands and my legs on the edge of the floor. I looked at the propeller. "Check in!"

"Check out!"

"Prop! Up! Down! Arch thousand!" I left the plane, but some-thing went immediately wrong. I started to flip, and I continued flip-ping. I didn't know which way was down and which way was up. My limbs were flailing everywhere. In one instant, the ground was in view, then the sky and the plane as it continued to fly on. Then the ground, and the sky again.

My training kicked in. We learned: "If you're flipping, arch your body, and you'll level out." I arched my body, bringing my arms to my side, my legs slightly bent while pushing my hips forward. I leveled out and became belly to earth. I lost count! "If you lose count, start your pull sequence."

"Arch thousand! Look thousand! Pull thousand! Check thousand!"

My canopy filled with air. Everything was okay. I didn't know what just happened, but I was safe again. I went through my checklist and landed safely on the ground.

In the video room, my fellow cadets and I watched my video. "You've got bad body position in the door," the instructor said. "Look at your hips, they're way too far back." We watched as my body appeared to tumble out of the plane. No form. No count sequence. No anything. Just a body falling to the earth. "I'm glad you arched and leveled out, but you can't flip like that," he said. "Rating level one."

What? Level one? I didn't understand. I flipped twice, but I opened my parachute when I was belly-to-earth. That was the safe way. I trusted the training. How did I fail? After the video session, I found Staff Sergeant Thompson, the head jumpmaster, and pleaded my case.

"Sergeant, I did what I learned," I said. "I flipped, but I leveled out and pulled at the right time. Shouldn't that be a level two? I don't think I failed."

"Parker, listen. I agree with you, but I wasn't your jumpmaster, so it's not my call. I've got to trust the other instructors. If he gave you a one, your rating is a one."

My failed jump meant I had to go to retraining for three hours. Everyone else who had successful or marginal jumps were lounging around, joking, and relaxing after a long, hard day. I had made three jumps, had nothing left to give, and now I had to get three hours of ground training to ensure I was fit to jump again. I was mad. I was angry. But I also knew what I did wrong. I had to bring my hips forward and bring my arms down to my side.

I'm standing second from the left. This picture was taken shortly after my flight landed on the ground. I had just failed my third jump.

I spent most of those three hours with an instructor in the mock-up of the jump door. "Prop! Up! Down! Arch thousand!" I yelled as I flung myself out of the wooden fuselage and landed six inches lower on the matted ground. I threw my arms down to my hips and arched my back as much as I could, pushing my hips forward as far as they would go. At the end of the three hours, my friends were in good spirits, but I was not. I was focused on the next jump.

For dinner that evening, I joined some fellow cadets, including Ryan and two girls we had met, to eat at a local restaurant just off the base. I was hungry, but I wasn't focused on the food. I was focused on my jump. Even as we ordered from the server, I wasn't paying attention. I must have looked strange as I continually went through the exit sequence in my head and threw my arms down to the side of my chair.

"Parker, it's okay, you can relax for a little bit," Stefanie, one of the girls, said to me. I tried, but I couldn't. For most of the dinner, I took a bite of my food, then practiced the exit sequence again, and again, and again. Back in my room, I positioned myself in the doorway and threw myself in the hallway, slapping my hands down to my thighs and thrusting my hips forward. At around eleven o'clock, I finally went to sleep. A 16-hour day with three skydives, having never jumped out of a plane before. Day one was done. Day two was hours away.

Less than six hours later, sometime between four and five o'clock, I was awake. Sure, I had the minimum crew rest with 12 hours of rest time between jump days and the opportunity for eight hours of uninterrupted sleep, but I was too nervous about my next jump. Jump four. I stepped into my olive-drab green flight suit and pulled up the zipper, put on my boots, and grabbed my blue cap.

This was it. One more failure and I went home without the basic parachutist badge. I'd have to go to every other cadet in Air Force ROTC at Ohio State and tell them how I failed the training and wasted the opportunity. All I could think about on our way to the drop zone was that failed jump, replaying it in my head. Poor body position in the door. Terrible exit. Flipping repeatedly. I couldn't do it again. Failure was not an option. I didn't want to disappoint my ROTC unit, and I didn't want to disappoint myself, knowing that, as a future Air Force officer, I wouldn't have the parachutist badge on my uniform.

"Flight manifests are up for the first three jump teams," Staff Sergeant Thompson said to us. "Have great jumps today. Freefall!"

"Freefall!" we all shouted back. I saw Ryan, who also made three jumps the day before, and walked with him up to the list. He was on flight three. I was on flight two. "You got this, dude," he told me.

"There's no other option," I responded. I was confident on the outside, but inside I was a nervous wreck. What if I failed? What if I returned to my unit without the wings? I walked to the gear room to get suited up for the jump. My demeanor was much more subdued than usual. I was entirely focused on my internal conflict. Could I do this? I had to do this. What if I failed? Failure was not an option.

As I was about to step into one of the leg straps of the harness, the jumpmaster for our flight walked in. He was wearing the signature blue U.S. Air Force Parachute team jumpsuit, but he was different from the other members of the team. He was short, stocky, and his grizzled face maintained a look that said he was pissed off all the time. He was a senior master sergeant, just one grade from being a chief master sergeant, the highest enlisted rank in the Air Force. On his name patch, in addition to the master parachutist badge, he also had the HALO badge. The set of wings that represented mastery in high-altitude, low-opening parachute jumps meant one thing: he was Air Force Special Operations.

And this man scared me. He wasn't relaxed and easygoing like the other jumpmasters. Staff Sergeant Thompson was from Los Angeles and had an easy-come, easy-go approach to life. Not this guy. He was all business, and he had to be. If you screwed around in special operations, people died, and not the bad guys.

"Listen up!" he barked. "Board calls! Everybody get crew rest? Anybody have alcohol?" he asked us, continuing down the line of mandatory questions posted across from us in the gear room. No one said anything. "Good! Follow me!" The doors to the flight line swung open, and we followed him to the tarmac to load in the plane. The sun had peeked over the horizon, allowing for full visibility on a perfectly clear, crisp morning. This is it, I thought. This is my last chance.

We made a few passes for other jumpers before it was my turn. I was the second jumper on the pass, so the other cadet got in the door first. I pulled down my goggles, which were affixed to my helmet, over my eyes, and adjusted my helmet. My eyes widened, and my mind went blank. I started to breathe more heavily as the jumper left the plane.

A few seconds later, the senior master sergeant pointed at me, directing me with his finger to move closer to him. I inched down the bench until I was next to him, standing but bent over and leaning forward toward him. He grabbed me by the collar of my flight suit, harshly, and pulled me close to his face, no more than four inches away. I could see his wrinkles, which I'm sure were caused by dozens of direct action combat missions throughout his career. Still holding onto my collar, he brought up his finger to my face, pointing directly at me.

"STAND!" he shouted, as he shifted his finger to the opening in the fuselage. "IN THE DOOR!"

In that instant, the hot September afternoon from 2001 flashed before my eyes. "That's it! I'm not doing it anymore!" I could hear Coach Miller yelling at me, embarrassing me in front of my entire team. "Every week you come out here and show that you can do it in practice, but you get in the games and you choke! You're a practice player!"

Practice player. I choked under pressure. I couldn't perform when it mattered, and here I was again, standing on a precipice in the sky, having failed my last jump. One more failure and I was out. I looked at the senior master sergeant, his eyes leering at mine with his finger pointed at the open door.

I was not a practice player. I would not fail. I had the training. I was prepared. I wanted to be there. I was motivated. I could do this. I must do this. I will do this. I was finally confident.

Carefully, I took the three small steps to the door. I placed my right hand inside the fuselage and my left on the outside of the plane. My feet, one in front of the other, were close to parallel with the open door as my toes inched off the edge. I bent my knees, pushing my right knee outside the fuselage. I pushed my hips forward as far as they would go. *Hips forward, arch, and throw my arms down and keep them there,* I thought to myself. If I could do that, I'd have a successful jump. I looked at the propeller, spinning at more than 100 miles per hour. I felt the wind across my body. I looked back at the senior master sergeant, who was holding onto the right side of my harness.

"CHECK IN!" I yelled.

"CHECK OUT!" he yelled back.

"Prop!" I yelled, as I looked at the propeller. "Up!" I brought my body slightly taller. "Down!" I crouched again, pushing my hips as far forward as they could go. "Arch!" I left the plane. I thrust my hips forward and threw my arms down to my side, slapping the outsides of my thighs with my hands. I arched my body as much as I could.

I looked up at the propeller, keeping my sight focused on the plane, now above me as I fell, to help arch my body even more. "Two thousand!" I kept my arms at my side as my torso began to align with my hips and legs. "Three thousand!" I yelled, as I began to bring my arms away from my legs and up to my side. I was now belly to earth. I did it. I didn't flip! I got it! But I lost my count.

"When you lose count, start your pull sequence." The training kicked in. "Arch thousand! Look thousand! Pull thousand!" My canopy opened and filled with air. It was beautiful and rectangular, and

I was flying straight. I conducted my checks and oriented myself to the drop zone, landing safely a few minutes later.

In the video room, the senior master sergeant started to review our videos. I watched intently as the VHS cassette with my name on it went into the VCR. He pushed play. I could see myself practically hanging out of the plane as I conducted my check-out sequence. I saw myself throw my arms down to my side along my hips and thighs and keep them there for a few seconds. I spun slightly as I started my pull sequence. The video ended about two seconds after my canopy inflated. The senior master sergeant didn't pause the video once or say anything as the video played. He only said two words after it ended: "Nice jump." He rated the jump a three and told me to manifest for my fifth and final jump.

It was all I needed to hear. I did what needed to be done. I was no longer a practice player. I finally knew what mattered: motivation, preparation, but most importantly confidence. I knew I could do it, I just had to believe. I believed in myself, and that belief—that confidence—is what enabled me to succeed.

Jump four was a success. Here I pose holding up four fingers with fellow cadet Joel Thornton.

I ran out of the video room to find Ryan and some of the others from my training group. Ryan's eyes lit up as I ran over with a smile. "You got it?!"

"Got a three, dude!" We high-fived, and I told him about the jump. He told me about his fourth jump, which he had done in the flight before mine. We walked over to check the manifest and saw that we were listed on the same flight. We'd be making our fifth and final jump together, just like we had started.

Having a new aura of confidence, I was much more animated in the gear room with our jumpmaster, a fourth-year cadet at the Air Force Academy whose last name was Dudley. Despite being only 21 years old, he had already logged more than 200 jumps. He had a big smile and seemed easygoing.

"I hope no one has had any alcohol in the last twelve hours," he said.

"Because if you have, that means you've been drinking on the job and you've got a serious problem," I shouted. We all laughed. Geared up, we followed Cadet Dudley out of the door. I was first behind him, which meant that I was first in the plane and would be the last to jump. Ryan sat two rows in front of me. As we ascended, he looked back at me and put up his right hand, spreading all five fingers wide symbolizing "jump five." I smiled, nodded, and returned the signal. As we leveled off, Cadet Dudley sent two jumpers out per pass. After the seventh and eighth jumpers exited the plane, it was just Cadet Dudley and me.

"Come here!" he shouted over the wind. "Check this out!" With his right hand, Cadet Dudley grabbed the metal bar that was mounted to the inside of the fuselage just above the jump door. Suddenly, he threw himself out of the plane, hanging on only by his right hand. My eyes grew wide, and I instinctually wanted to reach for him. He had a parachute on, obviously, but it was still unnatural.

His body dangled in the wind as it was blown up and down. He pulled himself back in the plane. "Wanna try it?" he said as he smiled.

"No way, man! Are you kidding?"

"Come on, it's fun! You'll love it!"

"I gotta make sure this last jump is a good one," I told him. It was my fifth and final jump, and I wanted to make sure I did it right.

"Suit yourself!"

When the jump light flashed from red to green, Cadet Dudley called me to the door.

"Stand in the door," he said, more calmly than any other instructor I had. Although I had overcome the challenge of my fourth jump, his demeanor was a welcome change from the other instructors. I took my position in the door. "Check in," I said firmly but softly, matching his level of intensity.

He nodded and smiled. "Check out." I began my sequence and left the plane. Again, I brought my arms down to my side, arched my body, and maintained a good belly-to-earth position. Despite pulling my rip cord a few seconds too early, I had a perfect jump. In those last few minutes under the canopy, I took a look around as I floated several thousand feet above the ground. Downtown Colorado Springs was off to the east, the Rocky Mountains to the west. In the distance I could see the famous Pikes Peak and several massive antennae coming out of another mountain peak. It was the North American Aerospace Defense Command, the organization that provides warnings of incoming space, air, and sea threats to North America. A lot of Air Force personnel worked there, and I wondered if any had graduated from the same program I was in.

I played around with my steering and made several turns. I was the only one in the air, so I had all the room to play around. I knew I had another successful jump, so I wanted to soak it in as much as I could. Around 1,000 feet, I entered my landing pattern, making several right-hand turns until about 400 feet when I flew straight until I pulled down on my brakes and landed safely on the ground.

I wrapped up my parachute and walked to the holding area for jumpers from my flight. The other eight cadets were there including Ryan, and another cadet named Joel who had been on my fourth jump. Cadet Dudley made his way over and called us to return to the gear room to drop our equipment.

"Cadet Dudley," I interrupted. "Do you mind if we get a picture?" I asked.

"Of course."

I posed with the other eight ROTC cadets and Cadet Dudley and had another cadet take our picture. It would be a keepsake I'd never forget. After watching the video and receiving another three rating on my jump, Cadet Dudley handed me the Basic Parachutist Badge. "Congratulations, Parker. You can choose any instructor to pin this on your uniform."

Posing with my entire flight, I hold up five fingers, symbolizing my fifth and final jump.

After thanking him and receiving my videotape, I walked outside, wings in hand, looking for the one person I wanted to pin the wings on my uniform, Staff Sergeant Thompson. "Sergeant!" I yelled as I saw him outside of the hangar. I ran over to him. "I have a request!" I opened my hand, revealing the metal wings. "I'd be honored if you'd pin these on me."

I stood tall and brought my heels together, my toes separated by a 45-degree angle. My hands were at my sides. My eyes looked forward. Staff Sergeant Thompson unclipped the backs of the two-pronged pin. Using his left hand, he reached inside the left side of my flight suit, pulling my uniform forward and making it taut. He With his right hand, he placed the badge about a half an inch above my name patch and pushed the pins through. He clipped the backs on each of the two pins, took a step back, and examined his work. "Congratulations, Parker," he said as he shook my hand. "Well done." Ryan had taken a picture of Staff Sergeant Thompson pinning the wings on me and had us pose for one more.

In the picture on the left, Staff Sergeant Thompson pins on my parachutist badge. In the picture on the right, my smile is beaming as we shake hands.

Two days later, I flew home, where my family picked me up and took me to dinner to hear about my training. While at the Star Diner, a family-owned restaurant that my family used to frequent before it closed, I sat across from my grandfather, who was wearing his signature U.S. Air Force Vietnam Veteran hat. I reached into my pocket, grabbed the shiny piece of metal, and held it in my hand.

"Grandpa, I have something for you." I brought my hand above the table, opened my palm, and revealed the wings. His eyes widened as he cracked a smile.

"Well, would you look at that," he said. "How 'bout that. I think that's pretty great."

"Grandpa, these are for you. They are the very wings that were pinned on my uniform a few days ago."

"Well, what are you going to wear on your uniform?"

"I've already gone to the base and purchased several more sets. I want you to have these. You were the first person in our family to earn a set of wings when you were in the Air Force, so I think it's only fitting that you now have the first set of wings from the next person in the family who earned them."

He took off his hat and scanned it. He unclipped the backs of the wings and pinned them on the center of his hat, directly below "U.S. Air Force" and above "Vietnam Veteran." He put his hat back on. When our waiter came to check on us, he looked at the server and pointed to his hat. "See these?" he asked. "These are my grandson's jump wings. And I couldn't be more proud of him."

Now, 15 years later (at the time of this book's initial publication), I look back on that fourth skydive: the senior master sergeant's finger in my face; his rough expression; his fierce words directing me to the door. And I think about how, in that moment, I recalled that late-September day when I was embarrassed by my football coach. I was called out for not doing my job when it mattered. I realized, in that moment, that the only thing holding me back from doing my job was me. If I could believe in myself, I could do just about anything. That was when I learned what confidence was and what it meant to me.

The dictionary has several definitions for confidence, but one strikes me the most: a feeling of self-assurance arising from one's appreciation of one's own abilities or qualities. But confidence is only one of the three pieces necessary for success; the other two are motivation and preparation.

If you want to do something: have the sufficient training to do it, believe that you can do it, and there is no doubt you'll succeed. From football to parachute training, at first I didn't appreciate my own abilities or qualities. I was motivated and wanted to be there. I was prepared and had the necessary training. I just wasn't confident. I didn't believe in myself. And as I mentioned several times in the story, I was scared. My fear was entirely rational, of course, as I could have been seriously injured in a football game or a skydive. The important point, I realized, is that being confident in myself and trusting my training actually *lessened* my chance of being hurt. Football and skydiving were serious activities that could result in major bodily harm or death, but the training I had was there to ensure I did the right thing at the right time and enabled me to keep doing it.

Today, not many tasks in my life involve the risk of serious bodily harm or death, but some of the things I do make me scared and nervous. And when those times come, I think back to that day on the football field and remember the practice player who was once me. I think about how I was motivated and prepared, but didn't believe in myself. Then I think of that moment in the plane, when I had a choice: pass or fail. Having all the motivation and preparation necessary, the only thing that would determine if I passed or failed was my confidence.

I also learned that **the fear of failing in front of others is a powerful motivator.** I could not imagine how I would have felt if I returned to Ohio State for my sophomore year without the parachutist badge. More than 100 other cadets would have looked at me and asked themselves the same question: "He went to Freefall, but where are his wings?" I would have been extremely embarrassed, just as I was on that day in football practice. That day was enough, and I never wanted to feel that way again.

This picture is a screenshot of the video of my fifth and final jump. My body is arched, and my arms are pinned to my sides. About two seconds later, I bring my arms up and start my pull sequence.

CHAPTER 3

THE MERCURY CENTURION: HOW SERVICE AND FAMILY BECAME MORE IMPORTANT THAN MONEY

Two discharges from two U.S. military ROTC units in six months hit me hard emotionally. But it was difficult on a more immediate level, too. It was April 2006, and I had less than a month and a half before I was set to graduate from The Ohio State University, but I had no job, no place to live, and no plan. I needed to do something quickly. I was a planner, and not having a plan was driving me crazy.

"Parker, this year has been really tough on you," my mom told me. "It's okay to come home and take some time to figure it all out." To her it was fine, but not to me. Living at home while jobless was not an option. About a week later, I found out about an "arts and sciences" job fair on campus and decided I'd see what it was about. I didn't let a little fact that I was a military history major with no applicable experience to anything outside of the military stop me.

I researched some of the companies who would be attending the job fair and found that most didn't specify a major, and that's when I quickly realized that the job fair wasn't about arts and sciences at all. There was no art or science. It was all about sales and sales positions. As a natural extrovert and former restaurant employee, I knew I could sell, so I just needed to determine the type of sales I wanted to do. My number one target, I decided, would be Ameriprise Financial, working as a financial adviser.

I knew it sounded weird that I was a history major applying to be a financial adviser. But in addition to my humanities studies, I had also been employed by Ohio State for two years as a physics, statistics, and math tutor, so I had a strong quantitative background. I was also lucky and grateful that my father taught me about investing and personal finance from an early age. I received my first investment, four shares of Nike stock, as a bar mitzvah gift. A year later, I made my first stock purchase with my own money, buying two shares of Lockheed Martin stock through my dad's broker. When I was 15, my grandfather and I both bought stock in The North Face Inc., as the company's signature Denali jacket was starting to go viral. By the time I was 16, I was analyzing my grandfather's investment portfolio. When I was 19, I opened a Roth IRA, which I funded with my own money, and got my first credit card. I opened a brokerage account when I was 20. With all of that combined, I figured I at least had a shot at landing an interview.

As the day of the job fair arrived, I put on the only suit I owned, grabbed my portfolio, and walked into the auditorium. I immediately identified the Ameriprise Financial booth and made a beeline for it. I introduced myself to a 30-something guy, who was tall, thin, and wearing glasses. I stuck out my hand. "Hi, I'm Parker Schaffel, and I'm interested in becoming a financial adviser with Ameriprise Financial."

"Hi, Parker, I'm Marc Miller, a manager with Ameriprise."

I opened with a line about how passionate I was about personal finance and how I loved to help people. "My ability to connect with people is one of my greatest strengths," I said. "And I think to be successful in any job you need three things: motivation, preparation, and confidence. As a financial adviser with Ameriprise, I'll have all three."

"If offered a position, would you prefer to work in Columbus or Cleveland?" Marc asked.

I hadn't given it any thought, so I put the question back on him. "Where do you think I'd do better?"

"Cleveland," he responded.

I told Marc that Cleveland sounded good to me and that I'd appreciate any opportunity regardless of the location. Marc told me some of the specific details of the position, the next steps in the application process, and the progression for obtaining securities licenses. He offered me a follow-up interview, which I graciously accepted, in late April at his office in Westlake, Ohio, a western suburb of Cleveland. While I finished the day with seven other follow-up interviews scheduled with the nine companies with whom I spoke, I was most proud of my interview with Ameriprise. I was excited about the opportunity, and I knew it would be the right job for me.

When I drove to Westlake for the interview, I noticed about eight other applicants waiting in the lobby. I did not know how many open positions they had, nor did I want to know. I was competitive, and I was going to come out number one because, as far as I could see, this was my only option, and the clock was ticking down before graduation.

The interview consisted of three parts: an in-person interview, a phone simulation with scripts and off-the-cuff conversation, and a computer-based assessment, which mostly tested for basic math skills related to finance. I enjoyed the phone simulation and breezed through the computer assessment. I passed each module and was invited back for the final interview, including a direct meeting and interview with Jeremy DiTullio, the Field Vice President for the Westlake office.

When I returned to Westlake two weeks later, I was sent directly to Jeremy's office. I walked in and saw him sitting behind his wooden desk huddled over a laptop. I knocked. He looked up and smiled. "Parker, come on in and have a seat," he said, extending his hand. I shook it and sat in the chair on the right side of his desk. *This is it,* I thought. *It all comes down to this.* We started the conversation with small talk, discussing our backgrounds and families. As we entered the substantive part of the interview, most of the questions he asked were standard interview questions, but one that stuck out was the last one: "Parker, why should I hire you?"

I had what I thought was the perfect answer, something my grandfather said to me a few weeks before when I told him I was interviewing with Ameriprise Financial. "Parker, the great thing about you is that when you tell somebody something, people believe you." It was a great compliment, and it meant a lot that my grandfather had that much confidence in me.

"Jeremy, I think you should hire me for two reasons. First, I have the motivation, preparation, and confidence to be successful in this position, and second, when I say things to people, they believe me." Jeremy sat back in his chair for a moment and cracked a slight smile. He leaned forward and lifted a folder that was open on his desk, exposing a sheet of paper, which he then handed to me. It was an offer letter.

"Parker, I'm happy to offer you the opportunity to be a financial adviser in this office, contingent upon your passing of the licensing exams." He smiled and put out his hand. "Congratulations."

I smiled. "Thank you, Jeremy," I said as I shook his hand. "Thank you very much. I really appreciate it."

"The thing is, Parker, because we've given you a commitment on the spot and are so confident in wanting you here, we feel that we should get the same from you, so we'd like an answer about this position within two days."

While a completely arbitrary timeline, I agreed to it. Only later would I recognize that he was playing to my emotions of the moment. But at that point, it didn't matter. I went downstairs and out to the parking lot to call my parents, grandparents, and a few friends to gauge their thoughts on whether I should take the position. About 30 minutes later, I walked back in the building and back into Jeremy's office. "Jeremy, I'm in."

My new quest was set. My new path was paved. Not only would I not be moving home with my parents as some jobless bum, but I had the career I sought, in a new city, with new people to meet. It was the opportunity of a lifetime. But it was going to be tough, as I would have to pass three licensing exams as quickly as possible, because, without the licenses, Ameriprise couldn't hire me. If I wasn't officially hired, I wouldn't earn a paycheck. Considering I signed a lease for a new apartment in Westlake that started in June, I needed the paycheck as quickly as possible.

On Monday, June 12, 2006, the day after I graduated Magna Cum Laude from Ohio State, my dad and I drove to Westlake to move me into my new one-bedroom, one-bathroom apartment. It was the first time in my life I'd be living alone, the perfect situation for me to study, day in and day out. After buying a bed, sofa, television, and dining room table, my dad flew back to Maryland on a one-way ticket.

In this picture, I'm hugging my grandmother shortly before leaving my apartment in Columbus. Moments later, I hugged my mom (left) and my brother (foreground).

Now, it was go time. I had the study guides, I had the motivation, and I had the quiet space I needed to get this done. First up was the Series 7 exam. It was the general stockbroker exam and the largest, most difficult exam I would have to take by far. Once I knocked that out, I had to study for and take the Series 66 exam, which would allow me to make interstate transactions. Then, I'd finish the summer with the Ohio life and health insurance exam. My goal was to finish all three exams by the end of August and start working by the beginning of September. The timeline was tight, but I knew I could do it. I had 10 weeks to pass the three exams. I was motivated and confident.

There was no mandatory class or seminar for the two securities exams like there was for the insurance exam, so studying for them fell squarely on me. The study guide for the Series 7 exam was 24 chapters and filled a two-inch binder with double-sided paper. I learned very quickly that there was a lot more to being a stockbroker than I thought. It wasn't like in the movies: a guy sitting in a big room shouting on a phone surrounded by his coworkers doing the same. I had to learn about stocks, mutual funds, bonds, call and put options, retirement accounts, and real estate investment trusts, including how to process all of them, specifics on how to make the transactions, and accountability.

A journey of a thousand miles starts with a single step, I told myself. Take everything one day at a time, one section at a time, one paragraph at a time, one word at a time. Every day between 9:00 a.m. and at least 5:00 p.m., I sat at my dining room table and studied. I'd take a lunch break, and a quick break in the afternoon to exercise, which usually consisted of a jog around my neighborhood. My apartment complex had a pool, but I didn't swim. I didn't have time to relax.

Day after day after day, I learned more and more and more. As my third week of studying ended, I called Ameriprise and asked them to schedule the Series 7 test on Friday, July 14. When the day came, I was as ready as I could be, armed with the knowledge I had shoveled into my brain during the past month.

I arrived at the testing center about 30 minutes before the exam started. The registration email told me to bring snacks and food, as the testing center had none available for test takers, and I was prohibited from leaving the premises once I started the test, a rule in place strictly to deter cheating. The test began at 9:00 a.m. and consisted of two sections of three-hours each and 125 questions, one in the morning and one in the afternoon.

I locked my mobile phone and food in a locker, and the key to the locker and my bottle of water were the only things I could take into the exam room with me. When I sat down at the computer, the proctor gave me paper and a pencil. I entered my unique login information, and the computer screen confirmed my identity. The first of two sections began.

The topics of the questions bounced from one to the next. One question asked about bond values, while the next asked about real estate investment trusts. Although there was no way to get my mind focused on one topic at a time, I knew that every question mattered and that a single question could make or break my final score. I needed to correctly answer 175 out of the test's 250 questions. Not a question less. If I was correct on 174 of them, I failed. If I reached 175, I passed. Failure was not an option. Success was my only choice. I knew I had studied enough. I was ready, and I knew I could do it. I finished the first set in the allotted time and took a 30-minute lunch break.

The second set of questions was no easier. One question at a time, one word at a time, I reminded myself. Just like I had studied. If I had time left at the end of this second section, I could go back and double-check any answers that I had flagged for extra review. When I finished the last question and was satisfied with all my answers, a screen popped up and asked if I wanted to submit my answers. I clicked yes. My heart beat faster. This was it.

Then another screen appeared. "Are you sure you want to submit your answers?" Yes. My heart beat even faster. My nerves on edge. Another screen: "Do you want to submit your answers for grading?" My heart beat out of my chest. A fourth screen: "Are you sure you want to submit your answers for grading?" I felt like I was going to have a heart attack, keel over, and die before finding out if I passed the exam. And that's what it would say on my tombstone: "Died of heart attack while anticipating his Series 7 Exam score."

YES, SHOW ME THE ANSWERS. I clicked "Yes" for the fourth time. The next screen appeared.

183 out of 250.

73%.

I passed. My smile wide, I leaned back in my chair and clenched both of my fists. My heart rate began to slow. I grabbed my scratch paper and pencil and returned it to the front desk. "You're all set," the woman told me. "Congratulations."

I opened the locker, grabbed my stuff, and went to my car. My first phone call was to my parents. The second was to Jeremy. "Jeremy, I wanted to let you know that I just passed the Series 7."

"Nice job, Parker. Congratulations. One down, two to go."

Looking at the breakdown of my grade, a note at the bottom indicated the national average score was a 73%. It looked like I was exactly average. As my grandfather always said, "If the average person can do it, so can I." And I had done it.

I went back to the books and studied for two more weeks before taking the Series 66 exam. The study guide was much smaller, and things seemed to make more sense to me, so I passed the exam with an 81% only two Fridays after I took the Series 7. The insurance exam was the final of the three tests I needed to pass, and the quicker I got this done, the quicker I could get to work. I took no rest, and I began my mandatory, five-day insurance training class the following Monday.

I walked into a large conference room on the first floor of a nondescript office building and sat down at a table in the front. A few minutes later, a retired MetLife insurance salesman named Don introduced himself to our class and began reading, word for word, the instruction manual created by his company, which supposedly contained 100% of the information that would be on the insurance exam. He broke up the monotony of the readings with personal experiences, in which he called some of his colleagues in the insurance business "jabronis," the somewhat mafia-esque word used for a buffoon.

We took occasional breaks and asked clarifying questions when necessary. The five days came and went, and I took another five days to study on my own before taking the insurance license test. Another Friday, another test. One hundred fifty questions later, I passed the insurance exam with a 75%. As before, all I needed was 70% to pass. The testing center took my digital picture and handed me a copy of my temporary insurance certificate.

Three tests in two months. I was proud. Very proud. I had done it. I did everything I needed to do. I studied hard. I focused. I stayed on target. I got after it. Now it was time to get to work. Jeremy and I agreed that my official start date would be Wednesday, August 30, so I took the last few days I had of foreseeable freedom to relax, exercise, and have some fun in the Cleveland area because I knew that everything would change once I started working.

In all my discussions with the working financial advisers in the office, I noticed the similarities in their advice. I didn't need a 100% on a license exam, they told me, but I did have to be a great salesperson, marketer, and advertiser. "You've got to acquire the clients." On the philosophical level, I had signed up to help people and ensure their financial futures. On the practical level, if I didn't have any clients, I wouldn't make any money and wouldn't be able to pay my bills.

Client acquisition was the key to long-term success, and Ameriprise Financial advisers focused on generating leads (and eventually clients) in two ways: through marketing and through their own personal networks. No cold calls. No phone books.

I was lucky and grateful that I had a large network through my family, friends, and the military, and while I didn't commission and officially serve on active duty in the military, dozens of my friends had recently commissioned and were making good salaries. I found that Facebook, still in its nascent stages, was a great way to connect with former friends from ROTC. Almost all of them, as well as some other friends and family, wanted to work with me. With about 20 initial client meetings already scheduled before I officially started, I knew that I would have a great first, second, and third week on the job. When August 30 came, I reported to the office in a new suit, one I had purchased for my first day, and sat at my desk, which was already set.

One of the first things I did that day was meet with my direct supervisor, a manager named John, a former Marine turned financial adviser. "Parker, it's great to have you here," he told me. "We're very impressed you've been able to schedule so many meetings already and hopefully acquire a number of them as clients." John then explained that every new adviser should have a client acquisition goal, and strangely enough it was the same goal for each new adviser.

"It's my job to support you in acquiring one hundred five clients in your first three years." John said that the statisticians at Ameriprise Financial's headquarters in Minneapolis had analyzed the numbers and determined that, if new advisers could acquire one hundred five clients in their first three years, then they were basically guaranteed to generate successful long-lasting financial planning businesses.

"In your first year, you should aim to acquire forty clients, then thirty-five in your second year, and thirty in your third year," John told me. "Aim for one client a week, and you'll reach this goal." I felt like I could do that, especially with my network and niche of potential military clients. If I had a good marketing plan, I could do even better.

Aside from my personal network and referrals, I learned that the other way Ameriprise advisers acquired clients was through its "lunch and learn" program, in which an adviser paid for the lunch of potential clients and would take the opportunity to give a small sales pitch to the attendees as the food was being prepared. Each attendee filled out an information sheet indicating their areas of financial concern, as well as their contact information, then the adviser paid the bill and left. Later that day, the adviser followed up with a phone call and discussed the attendee's financial concerns and built the relationship from there. If I could find a good restaurant and put my network to use, I knew I could be very successful.

Establishing these relationships, making hundreds of phone calls, and holding lunches were necessary parts of building a financial planning business. But they were difficult and unnerving, and it was easy to lose motivation. One bad day could lead to a bad week, and a bad week could lead to a bad month. One of the ways that Ameriprise Financial's managers motivated new advisers was through a weekly Monday morning meeting with Ted Jenkin, the Ameriprise Group Vice President for the Cleveland/Akron/Pittsburgh region.

Starting at 9:00 a.m., all the new advisers from the area would meet at his office on the east side of Cleveland, where he'd tell us about tips and tricks he used to be successful. He told us about times when he was down in the dumps and thought his career was floundering, but how he was able to pull himself out of it and become a Group VP and make massive amounts of money.

Ted had been in the business for some time and knew that money talked, and he put some money where his mouth was, bringing a bag filled with money to each meeting. Any adviser who acquired a new client in the previous week got to shoot a Nerf gun at a dartboard, which was filled with random numbers. Two clients earned two shots, three earned three, and so on. The Group VP added up all the numbers where the darts landed and gave that adviser the corresponding number of pulls from the money bag.

"Okay, hands up! How many of you got clients this week?"

My hand shot up along with some of my colleagues and others around the room. Then it was my turn.

"Parker, how many?"

"Six!"

"Six?! You acquired six clients since we last met?!"

I nodded. My colleagues backed me up.

"Wow. Okay. Six dart shots."

My six shots earned me 13 pulls from the money bag and more than $80 in cash. I got a round of applause and returned to my seat. It felt good to be recognized in front of everyone, and I was proud of how I was acquiring clients so quickly. My network was really starting to pay off.

The external motivators like money were powerful, but just as powerful, perhaps more so, were the internal motivators, like not looking like a failure to my colleagues. We were all competing against one another, not for each other's business, but to be the best in the office—the new adviser to get the most clients, bring in the most commission (ethically, of course), or generate the most leads. This competition was showcased front and center at twelve o'clock each Friday. All the new advisers, and some tenured advisers, would get together with a manager and report our numbers for the week.

Each adviser went through that week's numbers: leads, meetings scheduled, meetings met, clients acquired, and the commission we earned that week. The formula was simple: generate 30 leads and a get a client. Reporting zeros for anything, especially leads, was like a dagger to the heart. I could never imagine sitting there and saying that I generated zero leads for the week, which probably would lead to no meetings and no new clients. That scenario petrified me. I never let it happen.

As I completed my meetings with my initial network, I needed to establish a relationship with a good restaurant. Before the days of Google Maps and Yelp, most of us just drove around to find any legitimate restaurants we could. I found a great opportunity at a local, privately owned Italian restaurant called Arrabiatta's, located only a few miles away from the office. It was a good place, reasonably priced, yet still classy and open for both lunch and dinner. I met with the owners, and they loved the fact that I would bring people to the restaurant on a regular basis.

"Any business card or contact information I get, they're getting a free lunch for 10 people," I told one of the owners. "It's business for you and business for me."

As September turned to October and I had been officially working for about five weeks, I realized I was getting close to another goal of mine: acquiring 17 clients. John told me when I started that Ameriprise statisticians had determined that new advisers who acquired 17 or more clients in their first 20 weeks had a 97% chance of being successful in a long-term financial planning career, and advisers who did so earned something called the Mercury Award. In addition to receiving the award, advisers didn't have to work on Friday nights and could head out of the office around 5 p.m. Even better, Ameriprise had something called the Centurion Award, given to advisers who acquired more than 25 clients in their first 20 weeks.

Considering I had acquired six in a two-week period and was acquiring other clients left and right, I earned the Mercury Award in my seventh week and the Centurion a few weeks later. But I was working 60 hours a week, including 12 hours a day Monday through Thursday, nine hours on Friday, and three hours, and sometimes more, on Saturday. I was getting tired. Not only was I slowing down, but so was my business. The initial rush of clients I had from my network and my early marketing opportunities had come to a lull, and I found myself in a bit of a panic.

What happens if my business doesn't pick back up? Why am I not getting more clients? It had only been two weeks when things hadn't gone well, but it was enough to shake me. To keep my mind sane, which is difficult to do when work-life balance is limited, I joined the local recreation center and made sure I exercised at least a few mornings a week. I also made time to travel to Columbus for an Ohio State football game. A healthy body leads to a healthy mind, they told us in the military, and I knew that seeing my friends in Columbus for a game would help relax me.

In the next few weeks, I regained my motivation, thanks to a glance at my paycheck. Not only was I the first of the new advisers to earn the Mercury and Centurion Awards, but I was also the first to receive a large bonus: $4,000. It was the largest paycheck I'd ever received, by far, and I had earned it because of the success I enjoyed in my first few months. Ameriprise rewarded my success, and it felt so good.

A few weeks later, John recognized me in front of my colleagues and presented me with the "Top Gun" award, something he made up for our office, which lauded my ability to "target the right prospects, pull the trigger, and close the deal," as well as for the total sales I had generated, far more than anyone else.

While other advisers would have been complacent with the bonus and the awards, I wasn't. There was something else I wanted: an official, finance-related designation. All the tenured advisers in my office had one or more, and some of their business cards looked like alphabet soup from all the designations they had. CLU, LUTCF, AWMA, CMFC, and CFP. The one I wanted was the CRPC, the Chartered Retirement Planning Counselor. We learned early on that the baby boomer generation was starting to retire, and that meant the largest shift of assets in American history from 401(k) plans to Individual Retirement Accounts (IRAs). These people needed advisers to help them make the right decisions, and if I could earn the designation as a CRPC, I could really have an in with the retirees. Several of the tenured advisers in my office had the designation, but none of the new advisers did. I wanted to be the first.

I researched what it would take to get the CRPC designation, which consisted of successfully passing a test provided by the College for Financial Planning. Because it was December and business naturally slowed down for the holiday season, I would have more time to study. John and Jeremy supported my plan and said that the company would reimburse me the $499 that I paid up front if I passed the test.

Considering I was still working 60 hours a week, I knew I needed to factor in my study times into my personal schedule. As the Ohio State football season had ended (except for the bowl game) and the fact that I didn't have any friends outside of my work colleagues, I determined that my main study times would be the downtime I had in my schedule, including Friday nights and Saturday afternoons.

I knew I had to keep Sunday as a personal day to handle my other tasks and relax a bit, so I decided that I would also study in the early mornings on the days that I did not exercise at the recreation center.

The girl I was dating at the time, who saw me wake up early to study before I went to work, thought I was insane. I thought I was motivated. Much more motivated than others, perhaps. After studying through January, I scheduled the test for Monday, January 29, at noon. One of our administrative personnel set me up on a laptop computer in a private office. "You don't have any notes or anything with you, right?" she asked, doing her job as proctor.

I shook my head.

"Okay, then, good luck!" she said as she closed the door.

I began the 100-question, multiple-choice test on everything involving retirement accounts, including investment strategies, social security benefits, health care options in retirement, income streams, and tax planning. Everything I pumped into my brain from the study materials' nine modules was packed into 100 questions. I submitted my answers. Then I received the confirmation screen to show I had successfully submitted my selections, and my grade appeared.

Grade: C

Mastery: 70%

I smiled. It was all I needed. 70%. I passed. I ran out of the office and immediately went to Jeremy's office. "You're looking at the newest Chartered Retirement Planning Counselor."

"Nice job, man. I love it!"

Next, I stopped at our receptionist's desk. "Stephanie, would you mind helping me order new business cards?" I asked her. "I just passed the CRPC exam and would like to make sure the designation is on the cards when I hand them out."

The next stop was the bullpen to gloat to my other new advisers. "Watch out, boys and girls! New CRPC comin' in!" I knew they were envious. And that was a good thing. It's how the business worked.

In February, I had to get back on the client acquisition train and keep growing my business. Because I had many clients in San Antonio who were new U.S. Air Force officers, I decided to pay a visit to The Alamo City and meet with them, with the hopes of acquiring more business. Whereas most companies would pay for their employees' work-related trips, mine did not. But it didn't matter. I needed more clients. I had to get after it. I was just getting after it with my own money: $331 in airfare, $500 for a hotel room, $167 for a rental car, and hundreds more for lunches and dinners with current and prospective clients. The only reimbursement I would receive would be any business that I generated.

Pictured third from the right, I visit current and potential clients in San Antonio.

The money will come around, I thought, *as long as I get the clients.* My trip was filled with lunches with current clients, but I ensured they invited friends and other coworkers, scheduling meetings with them the next day to acquire the new coworkers as clients even before I returned to Westlake. By the time the trip was over, I had bought nine different meals for clients and prospects, but acquired four new clients in the process. When I returned home and went to work the next day, I told everyone how successful the trip had been, and that I was going to start scheduling follow-up meetings with new clients.

But as I met with each client over the phone, the meetings didn't go as planned. Three of the four clients were in poor financial shape. One new client, who was in navigator training, had debt that equaled twice her income. Another client donated so much money to his church that he had no extra income to save for himself. The more than $1,000 I spent on the trip barely yielded me any new business, and considering the financial outlook of my new clients, it didn't seem like it was going to happen anytime soon. Again, I got discouraged. If these were the new clients I was getting, I thought, how could my business go on?

I decided I would try another trip, this one to the D.C. area, which would allow me to see my family, as well as current and prospective clients in the area. But again, the trip didn't go as well as I had hoped. When I met with one set of potential clients, who were high-net-worth individuals, I didn't bring my A game, and they decided not to acquire my services. The following day, I met with another couple who decided to hire me, but when I returned to Westlake to process their paperwork, I found out they had given me incorrect social security numbers and had already tried to make a questionable transaction of more than $10,000. By law, I was required to report this to industry regulators to investigate as potential money laundering. Another trip and another subpar outcome.

What else could I do? I needed more high-net-worth clients but was struggling to find and acquire them. So, I went back to what I did best. In early March, I made another purchase for almost $700. It was the cost to obtain my next designation, the Accredited Wealth Management Adviser, the AWMA. It was more intense and complex than the CRPC designation, and it would take significantly longer to study for, but that didn't matter. I was going to get it, and once I had it, I could more easily attract the type of high-net-worth clients I was seeking. The books came in the mail, and I started studying.

A few weeks later in mid-March—I had been on the job for about eight months at this point—I got a phone call from my dad. "Parker, there's no easy way to say this." He paused. "Your mother has breast cancer." The doctors found it through a routine mammogram. It was early, but my mom required surgery, as well as chemotherapy or radiation, or possibly both.

I hung up the phone and stared at my desk for a few minutes and thought about what this meant for me and my family. My brother was only 14 years old, and my dad had a tough time handling significant emotional situations like this on his own. It was in those few moments that I had a paradigm shift unlike any other. My clients, my awards, my designation, my earnings: none of them seemed to matter in that moment. I liked my job, but my success had been waning in recent months, despite efforts to turn it back around. My work-life balance was still lopsided, and I hadn't made any friends on the west side of Cleveland other than work colleagues. With no outside life and no friends, I realized how important my family was to me and how they meant more to me than any job. I didn't want to leave them hanging for what would be a long medical process and months of recovery.

I assessed everything I had done in the previous eight months, and I decided to make a change. While I had been successful during my first year as a financial adviser—acquiring 40 clients and earning a designation—I wasn't entirely sure if I wanted to make it a 30-year career. At the time, I had no friends outside of work, and Cleveland was a rustbelt city only in its nascent stages of redefining itself. Although my two discharges from ROTC still stung in the back of my mind, my desire to serve my country was as strong as ever.

I researched the United States Intelligence Community, applied for a job as a military analyst at the Central Intelligence Agency, and was offered a position a few weeks later. I called my clients and told them I was taking the new job, explaining my reasons for leaving, and reassuring them that they would receive the same excellent service from my colleagues.

I moved back to the D.C. area in late May, a few days before my mom's surgery, and I officially resigned from Ameriprise Financial on my 23rd birthday, on June 26, 2007, just one year and two weeks after I moved to Westlake to begin my adventure.

It was the adventure of a lifetime, and I still am amazed when I look back and realize that I generated sound financial plans for dozens of clients in Ohio, Maryland, Virginia, Texas, South Carolina, Oklahoma, California, Florida, and Utah. I earned an official designation, bonuses, and praise from my managers. I earned the Mercury and Centurion Awards. And in that crazy year, I learned 10 valuable lessons, some of the most important lessons I've learned in life.

Never be afraid to pick up the phone and call someone. If I didn't make phone calls, I'd never schedule any appointments. If

I never scheduled any appointments, I'd never acquire any clients. If I never acquired any clients, I'd never help anyone. If I didn't help anyone, I'd never make any money. If I didn't make any money, I'd never be able to pay my rent. Not calling was not an option. Making hundreds of phone calls in a night was the only option. Bite the bullet, dial the number, put on a smile, and make the call.

Briefing and presentation skills can make or break your life. Once I got a client in my office, I had to be the most effective presenter out there. My financial planning business would live or die on my presentations. If I didn't make the sale, I didn't eat.

People buy on emotion. Nothing more, nothing less. I learned from the beginning that I could lay out logical reasons why someone would need a financial plan, a healthy retirement savings, and a rainy-day fund, but it never made someone take action. It was like trying to convince a smoker to quit based on the logic that he could get lung cancer. My clients knew logically that they needed financial planning, but it didn't drive them to do it. They needed emotion to motivate that action. Having a client understand that he needs money in retirement is a no-brainer, but having him emotionally describe the type of life he wants to live in retirement and then showing him how he wasn't on track for that type of lifestyle was much more persuasive. Emotion is the heart of why people make decisions, and it's important to remember that in business, family, and life.

Telling is not selling. The more I spoke, the less I sold. The most important thing, I learned, was getting clients to admit how they felt about their future. By admitting them, clients stated the emotional component necessary to drive their own decision making. Asking powerful questions to drive emotion was the key factor in enabling people to open themselves to obtain the help they needed.

Competition and envy are very strong, powerful drivers. The selection process for becoming an Ameriprise Financial adviser involved competition because our entire new hiring class was extremely competitive. Everybody wanted the one high-net-worth client, the diamond in the rough. Everybody wanted the one great restaurant that would give great lunches and great leads. Everybody wanted to report the most leads, most clients, or most commission at our Friday noon meeting. Everybody wanted to be the first to do anything. The competition was important because it kept us working hard. When someone else had a big success, we weren't jealous, but we were envious, firing the motivation within. "He just got a great client. How can I get a client like that for myself?"

Running your own business is exciting and scary. John and Jeremy told me and the other advisers from the beginning that our financial planning practices were our own businesses to run ourselves. Therefore, only being 22 years old, I was fairly autonomous. I generated my own leads, did my own marketing, and met with my own clients on my own. It was exciting, but it was equally scary. If I failed, I was the only one to blame. If I was successful, I was the only one who deserved the credit.

Confidence can lead the way, but you'll have to prove you're worthy at some point. I knew that I had to talk the talk and look the part. If I looked disheveled with a bad suit and a car that was missing a bumper, no client was going to trust me. If I didn't have enough money to look good and at least drive a decent car, why would a client entrust me to ensure that I could help grow their net worth? But as good as I looked, I had to back it up, and that was why I worked as hard as I could to get the Chartered Retirement Planning Counselor designation and start the process of becoming an Accredited Wealth

Management Adviser. The more designations I had, the more I knew, *and* the more people thought I knew.

You must have two of these three to be happy overall: a job you like, a place you like living in, and having friends and family around. There was no doubt I liked my job as a financial adviser, but I didn't like where I lived, and I didn't have any friends or family around. The relationship with the one girl I dated lasted less than three months. That time in my life only satisfied one of the three criteria. If you are close to family and friends and like your job, you can put up with a city you don't like. If you like your job and like where you live, you can be good without a lot of family and friends. If you've got friends and family around and like your city, you can put up with a job you don't like. In my opinion, no matter who or where you are, if you only satisfy one of the three criteria, you won't be happy. Having all three, of course, is the goal, but you've got to have at least two.

Have one or more goals and lay them out in short-, medium-, and long-term plans. Almost from the start of my financial planning career, I knew what I wanted to do and where I wanted to go.

In the short-term (first six months), I wanted to earn the Mercury and Centurion Awards.

In the mid-term (six months to five years), I wanted to earn the three designations of Chartered Retirement Planning Counselor, Accredited Wealth Management Adviser, and Certified Financial Planner, as well as become a manager in the company.

In the long-term (five years plus), I wanted to be the Field Vice President of an Ameriprise Financial office somewhere in the country. These goals kept me focused, especially when times got hard and I slipped into a lull, which can completely derail a person in a commission job. Everyone has bad days and even weeks, but I didn't let them consume me. When I had a week or two that didn't go as I had hoped, I went back to my strategic plan and regained my motivation to get back up, asking myself simple questions: What can I do today? What can I do in the next hour? What can I do in the next five minutes? When I broke down my situation like that, I reminded myself that one random phone call could land an answer on the other line that generated a new lead, which could lead to a new client. When I was tired of studying, I'd take a break but remind myself of my goals: be the first new hire in the office to earn a designation. My motivation returned. I'll never know if I would have become a Field Vice President, but I can rest knowing that, just before I left Ameriprise, Ted, the Group Vice President for my region, had asked me to speak at a conference for the region's top advisers. The topic of my presentation: how I acquired so many clients so fast.

Get after it. Never stop. Never quit. Never give up. No matter what I did, I always had to keep driving, keep digging, keep working. I wanted to be the best, the first, and to do that required a "get after it" mentality. When I told other advisers that I was going for the CRPC designation, they looked at me and said, "We've only been working for four or five months and you're doing that already?" Of course I was. I was going to get after it.

When I told others that I was going to pay the way for my own business trip to Texas, they said, "Well, I wouldn't go unless Ameriprise paid for it."

My response was simple: "I guess you're glad you don't have clients in Texas." It was my way of ensuring I stayed one step ahead.

Never stop. Never quit. Never give up. Get after it. That is the mentality I used to become the Mercury Centurion.

CHAPTER 4

THE SIX-YEAR APOLOGY: MY SERIOUS ERROR IN AFGHANISTAN IN 2008 AND CLOSURE IN 2014

I was on a plane flying to Afghanistan. It was August 15, 2008. I was 24 years old. Sure, I was young, but it didn't matter to me. I had joined the fight and was going to the war zone to help get the bad guys. I had no idea how unqualified, undeserving, and immature I was for the position, but I would find out during the next two months.

About three years before, I was on track to becoming a pilot in the U.S. Air Force, until a medical disqualification ended in my discharge, an abrupt end to my military career. My "service" consisted of three years in the Air Force Reserve Officer Training Corps, with about eight total weeks on an Air Force base. Nevertheless, my desire to serve my country in any capacity remained strong, and I applied for a position as a military analyst at the Central Intelligence Agency. I was elated when I received an interview and a conditional offer of employment a few weeks later. Following my background check and polygraph examination, I started working for the CIA on July 23, 2007.

Despite having a new career as a civilian, my longing for military service remained. When I found out that the CIA needed personnel to serve in Iraq and Afghanistan in a variety of capacities, I responded with immediate interest. On Friday, July 27, my fifth day on the job at the CIA, I came across a table next to the cafeteria advertising positions in Baghdad supporting the Office of Iraq Analysis. The banner on the table asked: "Want to go to Iraq?"

"Yes, I do!" I said as I walked up with a smile.

"And you're an analyst?"

"Yes, ma'am. Military analyst."

"Good, we need those in Iraq. When did you go to CAP?" the woman asked, referring to the Career Analyst Program, the formal, four-month training program for CIA analysts.

"Oh, I haven't been yet, I just started here on Monday."

The woman sighed. "Get in touch with us after you graduate from CAP. I'm sure we'll still need analysts then."

Wait until I finished CAP? I wasn't starting until December, wasn't finishing until next April, and this was July. That was almost a year. I couldn't wait that long. I had to get in the fight!

A few weeks later, a colleague in my office overheard me ranting about my year-long wait and handed me an unclassified pamphlet for something called the Crisis Operations Liaison Team. The pamphlet described COLTs as small cells of teams, usually one to five people, that helped pass relevant intelligence information to U.S. military units in combat areas, particularly in Iraq and Afghanistan. Because the job was purely liaison work, or so it seemed, I didn't need to spend a lot of time in training and preparation. I just needed to know the military, which I felt I did from my three years in ROTC.

After spending what probably was an unreasonable amount of time in my first four months at the CIA trying to convince management to let me take a position on one of the COLT teams, they cracked and said they would support me going for a short stint in the summer of 2008. I reached out to a guy named John, the COLT program manager, and met with him.

"Do you have any military experience?" he asked.

"Yes, sir. I was in Air Force ROTC for three years and have been to basic officer training, parachute training, and I've flown in the backseat of an F-16 before I was discharged for a medical reason."

Having only been in ROTC should have been a red flag to him, but I hoped he would support my participation. I didn't really have any true military experience, but my three years of ROTC training somehow met John's minimum qualifications, and he approved my participation in the program. The problem was that John was a field-based operations officer, one of the guys that lived overseas and collected foreign intelligence information. But he was serving a headquarters-based assignment because he committed a serious error overseas, was sent home, and was placed in that job. It didn't seem that he cared whether I was qualified or not. I was a warm body that fit into his schedule. I checked a box he needed, and that was good enough for him.

And it was good enough for me. I was bright-eyed and bushy-tailed. I was ready for the fight, whatever that fight was because I clearly had no idea. I had done little reading on the situation in Afghanistan before my assignment and could barely tell you the names of Afghanistan's provinces when I got on the plane.

I arrived at Bagram Air Base on a hot summer day and dropped my stuff in my "pod," a small Conex shipping container that was about 8 x 15 feet and contained a small desk, four closets, two bunk beds, and a 12-inch television. A shower and toilet room, which might have been 20 square feet total, occupied the end of the pod. Small spaces, sure, but I was ready to get Al-Qaeda.

In our work area, I met my boss, the communications officers, and the other personnel working at the base, including a few
members of the COLT team: Mike, an experienced technical analyst,
and Jeff, a counterterrorism analyst. While Mike and Jeff were serving longer assignments, my tenure in Afghanistan was significantly
shorter, which meant I didn't have a lot of time to show my impact
and leave my legacy. I had to work quickly and build relationships
fast. But I felt I was good at that. I was a schmoozer, and I could wheel
and deal. Just a year before this, I was a financial adviser, advertising,
marketing, and making sales presentations to dozens of clients. Even
better, I looked the part. I researched on the clothing to wear, and
I had it all: my 5.11-brand tactical cargo pants, U.S. Army combat
boots, American flag hat, and deployment beard, which I had been
growing for a few weeks.

My main job, as a COLT officer, was to attend various meetings
at the headquarters of the Combined Joint Special Operations Task
Force and ensure CIA information was passed to the military, and
that military information got back to the CIA. The main meeting I
needed to attend was the morning intelligence briefing to Colonel
Sean Mulholland, the commander of all Special Operations forces in
Afghanistan. Because I was going to be seeing him (and potentially
briefing him) daily, it was important to meet him as soon as possible,
so my boss introduced me in a one-on-one during my second day in
the country.

After some pleasantries, he asked the question I expected. "Any
military experience?" the man asked pointedly.

"Well, sir, I was in Air Force ROTC for three years in college,
but I was medically discharged before I could commission."

He smirked. "You'll find this is much different from ROTC."

Although Colonel Mulholland had been in the U.S. Army as long as I'd been alive, I knew I could do a great job. My military experience—three years in ROTC—was *certainly* good enough. I was in Afghanistan to beat the bad guys. I told him that I would work hard for him, attend his meetings, and ensure his intelligence teams had the information they needed. The meeting ended cordially, and my boss and I walked back to our work location, a little enclave of its own.

Each area on Bagram Air Base was its own dominion, almost like a base within the base. Each had its own badges and identification cards, dining halls, and recreation facilities, and Colonel Mulholland's Special Operations area was no different. If I was going to attend the meetings with the colonel, I needed to obtain a badge to his compound as quickly as possible. The badge personnel told me it could take up to a week. That meant I would need to be escorted onto the base to attend the meetings to which I was assigned. Luckily, Mike had an access badge and went out of his way to help me.

The next day, I was up early, energized, and ready to go. I walked over to Mike's pod around 6:45 in the morning and knocked on his door. No response. I started pounding on it harder and harder until I heard him rustle out of bed. "Hold on, man. I'm coming."

I knew he was sleeping, but I didn't have time for him to lollygag. I needed to be at that morning briefing! It didn't matter that he was helping me out and losing sleep because of it. This was my first full day, and this was important. We had to get going!

Mike and I walked down Disney Drive, the main thoroughfare through Bagram Air Base, named for a U.S. Army Specialist who died in an accident at Bagram in 2002, and arrived at the Special Operations area about 10 minutes later. Mike signed me in and sat with me through the first few briefings, helping me understand the lingo, acronyms, and operations that were being briefed, as well as introducing me to the major players with whom I'd need to work. After the briefings, we grabbed some breakfast at one of the dining halls and walked back to our camp so both of us could get to work on our various assigned tasks.

Mike woke up early for the next five days and repeated the process with me until I received my badge, one of eight total badges I would receive, and could attend the meetings unescorted. Mike was happy to get a little more sleep, and I was happy to be on my own.

By the end of my first week, it was clear that I had everything worked out. I woke up early and got to my work computer by 6:00 a.m. I'd compile the information I needed and head to the Special Operations area around 7:00 a.m. to attend the briefing at 7:30, sitting in the back-left corner of the wood-paneled room, between Major Matthews, a U.S. Army officer, and a guy named Larry, a liaison from the FBI.

The briefers ran through their practice briefings and made any tweaks before the final 8:30 a.m. briefing for Colonel Mulholland. After that, we'd all go to the larger operations center, where the colonel received a briefing focused on the previous day's operations. After that, I went back to my work location and handled the tasks of the day. I took a break around 3:00 in the afternoon to go to the gym and shower, and I returned to work an hour later to handle a few more tasks before I joined some colleagues for dinner around 7:00 p.m. I'd check my work computer one more time after dinner before I went to bed.

It was so exciting! There I was, in Afghanistan, fightin' the fight, passing information, and enabling operations. I had my deployment beard, my tactical pants, my combat boots, and my American flag hat. I felt like I definitely knew everything, and I was clearly doing a great job, even after a week. I must have been. After all, I was only 24 years old, with no true military or relatable work experience. What could go wrong?

About two weeks into the job, I attended the morning briefing as usual, and Major Matthews sat next to me on my left in his usual spot. "Hey, Parker. What's goin' on today?"

"Not much, Major. Another day in the sandbox," I said. "It's great being here. I'm happy to be a part of the fight."

"Yeah, you guys have a good team over there," he said.

"Oh, yeah, definitely, lots of great guys. Jeff is over at the 101st, Ryan is running comms all day, and Mike is doing . . . well, whatever it is that he does," I said, baiting him.

"What do you mean?"

Here was my chance to get a quick win with Major Matthews. I needed him to like me so his team, called the Special Plans Group, would quickly pass me the information I needed when I needed it. So, I did what any immature 24-year-old would do: I put someone else down to make myself look better.

"Well, Mike logs all of these working hours and all this over-time, but no one really knows what he does all day," I responded. "I mean, I certainly don't. We can see everyone else's time sheets, so we see how much he says he's working."

Major Matthews smirked, and the conversation ended as the briefing was about to start.

A harmless move, I thought. The problem was that Mike had been in Afghanistan for several months before I had arrived, and he had worked closely with Major Matthews, as well as Chief Warrant Officer Barnett, the enlisted lead for the military's intelligence analysts. As the new guy without much influence, their loyalties were to Mike, not me. Something I would soon find out.

About two weeks later, I learned that Chief Barnett's team went to the base's firing range from time to time. "Chief, I'd love to go with you guys," I said.

"Yeah, sure, Parker," he said. "We'll let you know the next time we go." But he didn't.

About a week after that, I was checking some emails on our base's special laptop, which we used to send information back and forth directly with the military.

"Who deleted the SOTF-73 Situation Report?" I asked my colleagues with a dash of attitude.

"No one deleted it," Mike said. "It had an urgent request, so I took action on it and archived it while you were at the bazaar."

While I was buying paintings, Mike was getting the job done. But I didn't ask him to do that. That was my job, not his. I hid my frustration, and we both turned back to our computers and kept working.

A week later, I was sitting in Chief Barnett's analysis center watching SportsCenter on one of the center's 20 or so televisions as I awaited the morning intelligence briefing. "Sergeant, you ready to brief on that piece of SIGINT?" Chief Barnett said to one of his analysts. He was referring to signals intelligence, a form of intelligence derived from electronic signals and systems used by foreign targets, such as communications systems, radars, and weapons systems.

"Yes, Chief. All set," the sergeant responded.

But that struck me. Why are they doing an assessment on one piece of SIGINT? I'd been a CIA military analyst for a *whole year* at this point, having graduated from the Career Analyst Program in April, and I had been trained in all-source, strategic analysis which used 10, 15, or even 20 sources in a single assessment. Even though I had no understanding of what was actually going on, using only one piece of intelligence seemed silly to me, so I smirked.

"You got somethin' to say, Parker?" Chief Barnett said to me. I was a 24-year-old former ROTC cadet who had worked at the CIA for a *whole year*. Clearly, I knew everything, and I bit on the chief's bait. "One piece of SIGINT, Chief? That's all you got?"

"You're damn right that's what we got!" he screamed back. "And our analysts are spot on!"

Headstrong, I dug in deeper. "Fine, if you guys are so good, then maybe you don't need the information I'm giving you," I responded.

"DO NOT THREATEN ME! YOU WON'T LIKE WHAT HAPPENS!"

The room went silent, and it was clear I had dug a very deep hole. In that moment, I might have kept digging, but I couldn't think of anything else to say. I sat back in my chair, turned back to SportsCenter, and awaited the briefing.

As if that wasn't bad enough, a few days after the incident with Chief Barnett, I hit the nadir of my assignment. I was arguing with Mike about something trivial, and Jason, one of the more senior officers on our team, intervened and told us to follow him outside. We sat down at a small metal table in our area's courtyard. Mike sat to my left, and Jason sat across from me.

"Something has to change," Jason said. "We can't keep having these arguments all the time."

"Fine with me," Mike said. "But Parker needs to stop talking about me behind my back."

Jason furrowed his brow, looked at me, and then looked back at Mike. "What are you talking about?"

"Parker was talking about my time sheet to Major Matthews over at the other camp, telling him I work a lot of hours but no one knows what I do," Mike said. "Everyone here except Parker seems to know what I do and how much work I have, including the boss, or she wouldn't sign off on my time sheet."

I had been caught in my self-induced situation, but as an immature 24-year-old male who lacked self-awareness, instead of owning what I did and apologizing, I dug in deeper and denied it. "Mike, I don't know what you're talking about. I didn't say anything about you."

"This stuff gets back to me, man. Don't you get it? I've been here a lot longer than you. You're going around telling people like Major Matthews all this stuff about me. Maybe if you wanted to know what I was doing, you should have asked."

"Mike, I didn't say anything about you or your time sheet." I continued to lie.

"Listen to me," Jason interjected. "Whatever the situation is, it's gotta get better because we can't have the constant bickering upstairs. You guys need to work it out."

"Fine."

"Fine."

My remaining few weeks at the base went by quietly as I kept my head down, stayed clear of Mike, and spent my free time with some other military personnel I had met. On my second to last day at Bagram Air Base, Colonel Mulholland, in front of his entire intelligence team, including Major Matthews and Chief Barnett, presented me with a wooden, hand-carved plaque with the Combined Joint Special Operations Task Force Afghanistan seal and an inscription praising my support to their efforts.

A picture of the plaque given to me by Colonel Mulholland.

"Thanks for all your work, Parker," the colonel said. "I wish you would have extended your assignment and stayed with us longer." Perhaps he was the only one who felt that way.

I stood up. "Thanks, Colonel. I've learned a lot being here, and I'll never forget all the work that you all are doing to keep up the fight. I hope to see you all again soon." Perhaps I was the only one who felt that way.

I went back to my base and showed my colleagues my war trinket, telling them about my plans to mount it in the center of my living room wall when I got home. Later that afternoon, my boss finished my performance report and sent me a copy. In addition to documenting the specifics of the work I did, in the last paragraph, she praised my patience, sense of humor, and my efforts to be a good colleague to everyone at the base. If only she had known the truth.

As the years went on, on the rare occasions I saw Mike walking through the halls at CIA headquarters, I gave him a head nod and kept walking. But as I matured and gained more self-awareness through journaling, experiential learning, and leadership training, the situation with Mike began to eat away at me. I recognized that I took the easy road, trying to win others over by putting him down, rather than the long road of building sustaining relationships through hard work and providing value.

In 2014, I ran into Mike on the sidewalk between the headquarters building and the parking lot. I was walking out while he was walking in. Normally, I would have cowered and put my head down, but this time was different. I wanted to set the record straight.

"Mike, do you have a moment?" He stopped. "I just wanted to say that I'm sorry for what happened at Bagram all those years ago. I shouldn't have said what I did, and I've felt bad about it for a long time, so I wanted to let you know that I'm sorry. I hope you can accept my apology." I put out my hand.

Mike looked at me and cracked a slight smile. "Thanks, man. But don't worry about it anymore. It was years ago. Water under the bridge. It's all good now." He shook my hand. "I'll see you around," he said as he headed into the building.

Since then, whenever I've seen Mike, I'm able to be at peace, knowing that, even six years later, an apology can do a lot of good to rebuild a relationship that never should have been broken. Mike was a great colleague and went out of his way to help me multiple times. He deserved an apology, and I owed it to myself to learn from that experience and know that hard work and providing value are the true ways to build relationships and earn respect.

True partnerships are not made, and leadership is not demonstrated, through putting other people down. Long-term partnerships are based on hard work, mutual respect, and trust. I didn't do any of those three, and I believe I hurt our organization because of it.

In many cases, you're not as important as you think you are. When I went to Afghanistan, I was a 24-year-old kid, with no relevant military experience and barely any CIA experience. I thought I was playing a huge role in the U.S. military's effort against Al-Qaeda and the Taliban, but I wasn't. And I wasn't, because I didn't have any of the relevant experience necessary to do the job. I had no true strategic understanding of the military's objectives or the intelligence it needed, and that was why my performance report mentioned only surface-level things, like "passing information" and "generating standard operating processes" for one of our separate computer systems.

It's never too late to apologize. While I can never be sure, by the time I apologized to Mike, I'm confident he hadn't thought about what happened in Afghanistan for years. But I had. And I think that's just how I am. I still feel like it was yesterday when my high school best friends and I had a huge blowup and never spoke to each other again. Through the situation with Mike, I recognized that these types of things from the past ate away at me and that I was apologizing not just for him, but for me. It didn't matter that it had been six years, or if it had been 10 or 20 or more. It's always appropriate to say, "I'm sorry," if you hurt someone.

Perhaps if I hadn't said those things to Major Matthews, it wouldn't have gotten back to Mike and Chief Barnett, and perhaps I would have had more cordial relationships with all of them. If Chief Barnett thought I was a good, respectful guy, perhaps he would have taken me to the firing range, like he did with my predecessor, and my predecessor's predecessor. Perhaps he would have been more understanding with me and my novelty in military intelligence operations. Perhaps if I hadn't been so ignorant and dismissive about his analysts' tradecraft, maybe he would have sat down with me to explain their processes and development of those assessments. Perhaps if I had learned all of that, maybe I would have been a better, more well-rounded intelligence analyst myself when I got back to work. But most of all, perhaps if I had owned up to my mistake when Mike confronted me, I wouldn't have felt as uncomfortable as I did for so many years.

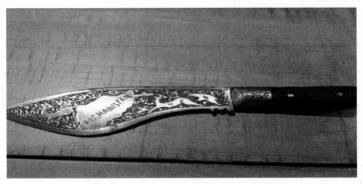

I purchased this engraved knife from the market as a trinket from my assignment in Afghanistan.

The parts of this chapter that describe me as omniscient and fully experienced are written satirically to emphasize my lack of self-awareness when I was 24 years old. The passages are written to emphasize my lack of understanding of my situation and how my lack of qualifications for the assignment were clouded by my desire to serve in a war zone and make up for my lack of true military service. I certainly did not know everything when I was 24, and I certainly don't know everything today. In 2013, when I was 29 years old and an officer in the U.S. Navy Reserve, I deployed to Bahrain and Jordan, satisfying my lifelong goal of deploying overseas with the military. All names of CIA personnel have been changed to protect their identities and I can neither confirm nor deny if any of these officers continue to work for the CIA.

CHAPTER 5

NEGATIVE TO POSITIVE: HOW MOURNING A TRAGEDY JUMP-STARTED MY MUSICAL CREATIVITY

I lived at the U.S. Embassy in Baghdad, Iraq, from August 2011 to August 2012. It was a transitional time for the U.S. and Iraq, as Coalition Forces had ended both combat and support missions in Iraq in December 2011. In February 2012, two months after Iraqi security forces had taken charge of their own internal security, two Iraqi parliament members publicly stated that emo and heavy metal music were Jewish/Masonic conspiracies brought to Iraq by the United States to brainwash and corrupt young Iraqi people. These young people, they said, sat in dark rooms, lit candles, and cut themselves. The parliament members said that the Interior Ministry's Society Police would investigate this problem and stop it. With little influence over the Iraqi security forces, we were powerless to stop it.

News reports circulated that up to 70 teenagers had been killed for their love of heavy metal music and the clothes they wore. Several other U.S. Embassy officers and I appealed to our Iraqi counterparts to stop the violence of the Society Police or any other armed groups against these innocent teenagers, but our efforts yielded no movement to stop the killings.

The issue impacted me deeply. I was an American, and I loved heavy metal music. We didn't bring this music to Iraq, nor did we corrupt these kids. I felt helpless. The only other thing I could do was pay tribute to these kids through a performance showcasing the same type of music for which they had been killed. Because I had shipped my music equipment to Iraq, I had everything I needed in my apartment on the U.S. Embassy compound.

I sent an email to my friends at the embassy, forwarding the news report of the kids who had been murdered, and asked them to come to my apartment that evening. I would play a show in remembrance of the dead. I was extremely nervous. I had never played in front of anyone before. While I knew it was the right thing to do, I had no idea at the time that my tribute to deceased, heavy-metal-loving Iraqi youth would lead me down a musical journey from timid musician to the front man of a heavy metal band to writing and recording my own original music.

I went back to my apartment and practiced three Metallica songs, ones I had known for years. Although I was nervous, I thought about the kids. It calmed me down. This was for them. My friends began to trickle in, grabbed some drinks from my kitchenette, and I began to play and sing. Some of the lyrics truly resonated with the moment. "Take a look to the sky just before you die. It's the last time you will," from Metallica's "For Whom the Bell Tolls."

"I can't remember anything. Can't tell if this is true or dream," from Metallica's "One."

"Creeping Death," from the eponymously titled song.

After each song, my friends would cheer and clap loudly, while understanding the reasons we were there. I felt proud that we would remember the kids that night.

After those three songs, we went to the British embassy for a party, invited by some of our colleagues who worked there. While walking through the crowd, I heard one of my friends who watched me play that evening tell some British embassy officers about my performance. One of the officers, a woman named Clementine, whom I had met briefly before, was impressed. She found me that evening, told me her birthday was approaching, and asked if I would play at her birthday party.

Me? I'd only played live once in my life, I thought, but the energy I felt was too powerful to overcome. I immediately agreed. A week later, I packed my gear and wheeled it over to another apartment for Clementine's birthday party. My set list included seven songs this time, four more than a week ago, a sign that I was already more confident. I played some of the same Metallica songs, but added songs from other heavy metal bands, as well as some alternative rock bands.

Just as the week before, the audience was impressed, and I was incredibly humbled. It was my second performance in front of people in as many weeks, and I felt a new sense of energy. I loved being in front of people, and I loved playing live. Those who had seen me play were telling others around the embassy how good I was, and it felt great to be the subject of others' praise.

As word spread about my two performances, a colleague at the embassy came to my office. She had been spending a lot of her personal time with a contractor named Kevin, who worked at another U.S. compound down the street from the U.S. Embassy. "He loves metal, too," she told me. "You should definitely meet him."

Kevin and I met a few days later and discovered that we had the things that mattered most: a love for heavy metal and access to guitars and amplifiers. We exchanged phone numbers, and Kevin came to my apartment a few nights later to play. From the beginning, it seemed like we would work out just fine. Every song I knew, he knew, including songs from bands like Metallica, Slayer, Megadeth, Offspring, and Godsmack. And Kevin was a great guitar player, too; his guitar solos were clean and on point.

The more we practiced in my apartment, the more people began to hear about our twosome. We seized the moment of popularity and agreed to put on a show for the entire embassy. We decided on a nine-song set list and organized the event, which we would hold at the pavilion by the embassy's pool. It was a large space with tables and chairs, and a 20-foot-long wet bar in the back, the perfect spot for some live music. I booked our audio/video staff to set up the PA system and made flyers to further promote the event.

This is the flyer, made in Microsoft PowerPoint, that we used for our first show.

The night of the show, Kevin and I helped set up the stage and got ready to play. I gave an iPod, preloaded with our set list, to the guy running the PA system. Although Kevin and I were both playing guitars and I was singing, we had neither a drummer nor a bass player, so we needed the drumbeats and other backing tracks of the original songs to provide extra support.

When it was time, people began to show up, and many seemed in disbelief that a show like this was actually happening. There had been plenty of live music shows at the U.S. Embassy before, but most played country music or something much softer than our set. Kevin and I played our nine songs and had a great time. We got some hearty applause and cheers of support from the crowd, around 50 people. No one was headbanging in front of the stage, but people seemed to enjoy it. We were proud that we could put on a good show for the embassy. I thought again of those kids who had died just a month before. This was for us, but it was also for them. We had brought heavy metal to a large stage in Baghdad. There was no conspiracy and no corrupting Iraqi youth. It was a good show, with good people, and good music. And that's what it was all about.

After the show, Kevin and I were talking when a guy came up and introduced himself. "Hey, guys, I'm Eric," he said. "I thought tonight was great, but I wanted to let you know that I can play the drums to every song you just played." *Yeah, right*, I thought to myself. *No way could this guy play drums to our songs.* Our songs were really hard songs to play on drums and the odds that this guy could play them were extremely low. But I thought it was worth a shot. "If you're serious, it sounds good to me," I responded. Kevin nodded. I gave Eric my phone number.

A few days later, Eric came over to my apartment. Kevin couldn't make it because of some work he had to finish. "Alright, what do you think?" I asked Eric.

"How about 'Seek and Destroy'?" he said, referring to a famous Metallica song. I love the song. It's fun to play and has a great chorus that audiences love to sing. Eric sat at my electric drum set, and I plugged my guitar into my amplifier. The song starts off with only a guitar riff, so I began playing. As I finished the fourth measure, Eric joined in on the drums. We started playing together. Within the first minute, I knew we had something special. It was an energy that flowed between us. It was like we knew what each other was going to do and when we were going to do it. We made it through the whole song without stopping, a true feat for two people playing together for the first time. I was sold. I immediately called Kevin and told him the news. "Dude, you have to get over here."

"Really? It was that good?"

"Yes. It was *that* good."

Kevin obliged, finished his work, and came over about 20 minutes later, joining Eric and me for one song before we called it quits for the night. Kevin was equally impressed with Eric's drumming. We had our trio, our *band*. I had never been in a band before, but I was excited. I couldn't believe that the three of us had found each other, and it all started because I wanted to remember those Iraqi kids.

From that point on, a few nights per week, Kevin and Eric would come over to my apartment and we'd practice for an hour. The more we played, the more I found out that Eric wasn't kidding about being able to play what Kevin and I could. Every song Kevin and I played, Eric could play. When Eric couldn't practice with us, he practiced in his own apartment, using his mattress, pillows, and stacks of books as his makeshift drum set. Kevin practiced at his place with his guitar and amplifier, and I did so with mine. It was all coming together.

The energy I felt from playing those first shows, at first by myself, and then with Kevin, grew stronger, and I wanted to play more. Kevin and Eric had been in several bands before, so they didn't need any convincing to play live. Having already played at the pavilion, we thought a great place to play would be the Marine House—where all the members of the Marine Security Guard (MSG) detachment lived. The MSG were young, rambunctious, yet professional. They were great at their jobs, but also threw great parties. We talked with the MSG detachment commander, a gunnery sergeant, who was fully on board with our idea to set up a stage in their bar area and put on a metal show. "Marines love metal," he told us.

With only a few weeks until the event, we started working on a flyer, but realized something was missing: a name. We were a band, but we didn't know what to call ourselves. "Baghdad Heavy Metal," which we used on the first flyer, wasn't good enough, so I thought about it. I thought back, again, to how this whole thing started. Eric met us because Kevin and I played together. I met Kevin because the girl he was dating heard about my playing at Clementine's birthday party. Clementine invited me to play at her party because she saw me play my first show in my apartment. I played that first show in memory and mourning of those Iraqi kids who were slaughtered because they listened to heavy metal music. They were singled out by politicians who called the heavy metal music an American conspiracy. That was it. I had it. Heavy metal. Conspiracy. America. American Metal Conspiracy was born. It was our tribute to the dozens of Iraqi kids who lost their lives to senseless, archaic, draconian violence.

The American Metal Conspiracy Logo.

The day of the event came, and it was our time to rock and roll. Eric and I booked the embassy's audio/video team and had the stage set up, and Eric borrowed an old crappy drum set he found in a closet in a rarely used part of the embassy. Apparently, it had been used as part of church services and survived the eight prior years of warfare. We checked our levels and watched as the crowd came in. With each new person in the door, I grew more nervous. I had never played for this many people before. What if I made a mistake? What if I forgot the lyrics?

I thought back to my time on my high school football team, that day of being called a practice player. I had practiced these songs plenty, and I wanted to play the show. I was ready to play this show. I just needed confidence. I remembered that day from football practice and those skydives I made years before. I could do those things, and I could do this. I focused. So what if I made a mistake? So what if I forgot a lyric? I would do my best. It was all I could do. After my internal pep talk, I had the confidence I needed. I was motivated, prepared, and confident. I was nervous, but that was a good thing. It meant that I was about to do something important. If it wasn't important, I wouldn't be nervous. I was putting myself out there, vulnerable, in front of about 75 people. It was time to start. The nerves could wait.

We opened with an explosive start to the Metallica song "Creeping Death." Eric started the drumroll, and we broke into the song with a drum crash and Kevin's guitar. I belted out the lyrics. Some people smiled, some cheered, and some were clearly surprised at what was happening. We were doing it, and it was sounding great.

We played the rest of the songs on our set list, making plenty of mistakes along the way. I certainly noticed them, and the crowd might have too, but it didn't matter. We were crushing it. For our second-to-last song, we invited one of the MSG Marines on stage to sing the lyrics to Rage Against the Machine's "Killing in the Name." It was clear that we made the right choice in having a Marine sing it, as every other Marine in the place went bonkers when we played the song. At the end of the night, people repeatedly asked us when we were going to play next. While we didn't have anything on the books, we took the feedback as votes of confidence to get something going soon.

That night, back in my apartment, I reflected on that night's events. I realized I loved playing for others. It gave me an incredible rush. Standing on a stage with a microphone, I discovered that I could command a crowd. I instinctually knew what to say and when to say it and knew when to get the audience into a song. An extreme extrovert, I got my energy from other people, and being center stage let me do that. I loved it. Keeping the "conspiracy" alive, we scheduled our next show three weeks later, on June 9, the day before I was scheduled to go on my third and final three-week rest period out of Iraq. As Kevin and Eric also had upcoming rest periods after mine, it was likely to be our final show.

Kevin, Eric, and I met and agreed to double our set list, adding music from several new bands, and we decided to hold the show back at the pool pavilion. We advertised and practiced hard. I wasn't a member of a band back home, so as far as I was concerned, this could be my last show ever. I wanted to make sure I played in style. I had a coworker buzz my hair into a Mohawk.

With about 100 people there, it was the largest crowd we had. Many had come to our previous shows, while others were looking for something to do that night. We opened with a popular song by AC/DC, one of the new songs on our set list. We played hard and fast and ended our first of two sets with "One," my favorite song by Metallica. While I played the opening guitar riff, I heard a loud whistle from the back of the pavilion. I looked up and saw a guy with long, curly black hair standing with his fist in the air. I smiled and gave him a nod as I continued to play. We broke into the main part of the song, getting heavier and faster. Kevin's and my guitars sounded like one instrument. Eric's drumming was tight and on beat. We were head-banging. It was awesome. I ripped into the two solos to end the song, receiving cheers from the crowd as I played them, and ended the song with two blasting beats. It was the greatest I had ever played the song, and I did it in front of dozens of people. We got a huge roar of applause and cheers from the crowd, especially the guy in the back who had whistled.

After about a 10-minute break, we started our second set with a song called "Awake" by Godsmack. The moment Eric hit the crash cymbal that entered us into the song, the same guy with the long, curly black hair who was standing in the back of the room charged the stage and started headbanging like he was possessed. He was throwing his head to and fro, his curly hair whipping around. I watched him from the stage as I continued to play. How incredible, I thought to myself. Here I was in Baghdad, Iraq, playing music that I loved, and someone else was enjoying it just as much. I was express-ing myself through music, and he was expressing himself through headbanging at the front of the stage. This is what music was about. I thought again of the kids who died and how much they loved music like this too.

We kept playing the remaining songs of our set, and the head-banger and a few of his friends would come and go. Our set ended with some crowd favorites, and I was able to get just about everyone in the pavilion singing along. We finished with AC/DC's "Highway to Hell," a fitting tribute, we figured, as Iraq was still facing car bombs and other violent incidents on a regular basis. As we finished the song, the crowd gave us a standing ovation, and many of them came up to the stage to give us high fives and words of gratitude.

After we finished, we helped take down the stage and remi-nisced about how far we had come in just a few months. The next day, I left for my three-week rest period. It was the last show I ever played with American Metal Conspiracy. As a parting gift to my bandmates, I had a local Iraqi embroider three, small black flags with our names, the instruments we played, the band name, and our makeshift logo. Our names and instruments were written in both Arabic and English. At the bottom of the flag was our tagline: "Baghdad Heavy Metal."

Until March 2012, I had never played for a crowd before and now I had played three live shows in a band in as many months. It was clear that I found something I was truly passionate about, and it all started because I wanted to pay homage to those Iraqi kids. I made it a personal goal to join a band when I got back home.

American Metal Conspiracy. Left to right: Eric, me, and Kevin.

In December 2012, a few months after I returned home, I posted an ad on Craigslist: "Metal vocalist/guitarist looking for metal band." I explained that I was into heavy metal, played rhythm guitar, and could sing at the same time. It was something not many people could do well, so I hoped my niche would land me somewhere.

A few days later, I received a response from a guy named Herb, who said that he played with a few guys in his basement on Friday nights. He invited me to join. In January 2013, I went to Herb's house on a Friday night. I didn't know what to expect, whom I'd meet, or what we'd play. But I was willing to give it a shot because I wanted to be in a band. I wanted to be on stage.

I drove to Herb's house in a tucked-away, dark street in Annandale, Virginia, about 10 miles outside of Washington, D.C. I knocked on the door with my guitar in hand. Herb answered and introduced himself. He was shorter than me but had a strong build. He wore a baseball cap and glasses. He led me down to his practice space, a small area in his basement, where the previous owner had created a recording studio. Herb, I found out early, was an incredible guitar player. His fingers moved quickly and smoothly along the fretboard, like magic. I had never played with anyone as good as him. No matter what, I wanted to continue playing with him.

I must have impressed Herb on some level because he invited me back the next week. After a few weeks of playing with him and two other guys, Herb pulled me aside.

"George and Ryan, they're good guys," Herb said, "but they're not into the same kind of music we're into." I agreed. "I'm not going to invite them back next week, and I'm going to start searching for a bass player and a drummer."

As 2013 progressed, Herb stuck to his word and found not just a bass player, Carlunle, and a drummer, Carlos, but a third guitar player, Chuck. By the end of 2013, we had our five-piece group, all guys who loved heavy metal and all guys who wanted to play live shows.

We settled on the name Death Echo, something I came up with randomly, and practiced every Thursday night, focusing our set list on songs from the best metal bands from the 1980s: Metallica, Slayer, Megadeth, Anthrax, and Exodus.

The Death Echo logo as designed and digitized by Mark Riddick.

After months of practice and rehearsals, we were finally ready. "I think I found a place we can play," Herb said at practice one night. "It's called the Grog'n'Tankard. Their website says they have live music and they have all kinds of bands play." I reached out to the owner and met him at the venue, located in Stafford, Virginia, about an hour south of Washington, D.C. The venue turned out to be a large, old house that was converted into a bar and a small stage, about eight inches in height.

"Yeah, we definitely want you guys to play here," the owner who went by Hoss told me. "We have a great metal crowd that comes up from Fredericksburg, about a 10-minute drive. This place will be crazy if you guys play." Hoss booked us with two other local bands.

"Guys, we're booked at the Grog," I emailed my band later that day. "They say they've got a good crowd, so it should be good to grow our fan base."

When the day came and we drove to the show, we found that the only people there were the other two bands and the few family and friends we had brought with us, about 10 people.

I belt out the lyrics as my other band members chug along during a show at the Grog'n'Tankard.

But it didn't matter. We played, and we played well. It was just like being in Baghdad. I was playing the music I loved in front of people I care about and people who cared about me. And in the end, we had fun. We played at the Grog a few more times, despite the lack of a legitimate crowd, adding several other locations in the Washington, D.C., area to our venue list.

Death Echo playing at The Pinch, a dive bar in the Columbia Heights neighborhood of D.C.

Around the same time, I was introduced to the Patricia M. Sitar Center for the Arts, colloquially called the Sitar Arts Center, which provides multidisciplinary arts education to underprivileged children in Washington, D.C. They needed more instructors, and I was looking to give back to my community, especially to those who had less than me. My passion for community service grew after I returned from Iraq, having seen how the U.S. Embassy's Office of Cultural Affairs positively impacted communities throughout Baghdad through arts outreach to local Iraqi youth and their families. Those Iraqi children had very little, and a lot of kids in D.C. were the same way.

I began instructing in January 2015. My first class was a group of five kids ranging from 11 to 16 years old. None of them had ever touched a guitar before that class, and it was my job to teach them a skill that could last them a lifetime. Into February, March, and April, I taught the students different chords, strumming techniques, finger positions, and how to tune their guitars. In May, the students performed at the Student Showcase, putting their newly learned talents on display for their families, other students, and Sitar staff. I'll never forget the moment they took the stage, all sitting in a row with their guitars in hand.

The oldest of the students counted off, and they began to play a song they made from the chords they learned. The students strummed in rhythm, switched chords simultaneously, and finished with a crescendo of sound before standing and taking a bow. Watching them, I shed tears of joy. Five months before this, these students had never played an instrument and now they were performing in front of an audience. I thought about how happy they were, despite being nervous, and how proud their parents must have been. I was proud, too. The beauty of music is that it is truly the international language. No matter where these kids went in life, an E chord on the guitar was an E chord on the guitar. They would always have this skill as long as they lived.

From 2014 to 2016, I continued teaching at Sitar, adding new students to my guitar classes each semester. I also continued playing in Death Echo. While I loved Sitar, its children, its staff, and what it did for the community, Death Echo started to stagnate, and in late 2016, Herb and Carlos branched out and played in other bands in addition to playing in our band.

At the same time, I started thinking that it wasn't enough for me either. While playing other bands' songs had been fun, it started to get boring. But I didn't have much motivation to learn new songs. My bandmates and I had talked about writing original music, but as a whole we didn't have the same motivation to compose our own songs.

Around that same time, an event in November 2016 ignited something inside me and catalyzed me to write my own music: the election of Donald Trump. I didn't pay attention to the news on election day. I voted in the morning, went to work, and then went to a hotel/casino in West Virginia with my then-fiancé, now-wife Abby to get away. We had dinner, gambled, and watched HGTV before we went to sleep. I didn't find out the results of the election until the next day.

When we returned home, we found our neighbors distraught. Anger raged in many, and I could appreciate why, but I was willing to give Donald Trump a shot. I agreed with what Hillary Clinton said in her concession speech: "We must give Trump the chance to lead."

As I dealt with my own emotions with what was happening, my anger, fear, and downright concern for America's future hit their peaks. Although I journaled about my emotions, it wasn't enough, so I did something I had never done before. I started to write song lyrics. I didn't know what they would turn into, but I wrote them nonetheless. To my surprise, writing lyrics came easily, and I started to find themes in my words. I wrote lyrics to a song about Trump's overwhelmingly white, male, and excessively rich cabinet members; his use of Twitter as a platform for verbal warfare; and the increasing potential for nuclear destruction.

When I read through the lyrics, they seemed to have an underlying rhythm, so I grabbed one of my guitars and came up with a few riffs. Some sounded good, so I recorded what I was playing on my phone. Then I'd replay the video, sit at my drum set, and play along. But it wasn't enough. I wanted to truly make something of what I was doing. I wanted to make a statement to the United States and the world. I wanted my new music out for the masses, but I had no idea how to record music or how to get it published.

I contacted Mark Riddick, a guy I met at a local metal show a few years back and a guy with whom I kept in contact. Mark was a world-famous heavy metal artist and had designed the Death Echo logo and T-shirt. But more importantly, he self-recorded his own heavy metal project called Fetid Zombie, so I figured he'd have some insight into what I should do. We met for lunch one Saturday, and he told me everything I needed to know, including the hardware and software to buy, as well as some dos and don'ts of recording. After our lunch, I went home and purchased everything. My home recording studio was set up in less than a week.

Over the course of late December 2016 and early January 2017, I went to work recording the five songs I composed, but it was extremely difficult. I learned early on that I had to record a single guitar riff 30, 40, or even 50 times to get it right and mostly error-free. I also quickly learned that Abby's support was critical to keep me going. When I'd get frustrated from repeatedly making the same mistake, she'd calm me down. "I'm proud of you," she'd say. "I think it sounds great." She enabled me to regain my patience, calm down, and keep going.

While I learned the basics of how to record songs from my software's tutorials, I had no idea what to do with them once they were recorded, so I contacted a Massachusetts-based amateur audio engineer named Ben Schwartz, a guy Herb knew, to see if he wanted to support my project. I sent him an email on January 3, and by the next night Ben sent me a mixed draft of my first song and offered to mix and master my entire five-song album for a small fee. We agreed, and Ben went to work. With the music recorded and an audio engineer on board to mix the tracks, I was missing one critical thing: a name.

I decided that I didn't want to release the music under my own name—that was more for singer/songwriters who played pop music—so I had to come up with a band name, just like Mark had done. I found my inspiration in the 1988 Metallica album entitled ...And Justice for All. It was a politically themed, hard-hitting, heavy metal album, one that I grew up listening to as far back as elementary school. I had been listening to it a lot again, considering the current political situation, and started to read some of the lyrics.

In the third verse of the lyrics to the eponymously titled song, something jumped out at me. "Lady Justice has been raped, truth assassin. Rolls of red tape seal your lips, now you're done in. Their money tips her scales again, make your deal. Just what is truth? I cannot tell, cannot feel." It was right there, the perfect name for my project. Truth Assassin.

Before I got too excited, I scoured the web for anything related to the name Truth Assassin and found nothing major related to copyrights or other bands, only a few references to a video game, a television show, and the stage name of a magician in Brooklyn. That was the day Truth Assassin was born. I called Mark to tell him the news, and he agreed to create a logo for Truth Assassin. Within a few days, I had received some draft designs and selected my favorite.

The Truth Assassin logo, as designed and digitized by Mark Riddick.

It was all coming together. I had recorded all the music and decided on a name; Ben had mixed and mastered the songs; and Mark had created my logo. The last step in the process was selecting the distribution company to get my music to the world. I found one that supported independent artists like me, called CDBaby. I paid for its service, submitted my music for a copyright, and released it on January 20, 2017, Donald Trump's Inauguration Day.

I called the album *The Scourge.* I used music to stand up against hatred and bigotry five years ago when I was in Iraq, and I was doing the same thing again. Abby and I spent Inauguration Day in Richmond, Virginia, and made the trip via a two-hour ride on an Amtrak train. I emailed my friends and family, informing them of the release:

> *I want to share something I'm very proud of: my very first solo music project called Truth Assassin. During the past five weeks, I've recorded guitar and bass riffs, drums, and I've written lyrics, and the like. I put them all together and came out with five songs on an album called The Scourge. Three of the five are punk, one is metal, and one*

*is instrumental with piano and acoustic guitar. If you're in
the mood for some cathartic music today, I encourage you
to check it out. Even if the lyrics don't resonate with you, I
hope you can appreciate the music.*

Some were gracious enough to download it on iTunes or listen to it on Spotify and let me know what they thought. "This is awesome!!! Congrats and thanks for sharing!" one of my cousins emailed. "Really thoroughly enjoyed it and will listen on as we begin our resistance to this insanity," my neighbor responded.

A few weeks later, I married my wonderful, beautiful, amazing wife Abby, and took a few months to establish a strong foundation of our marriage. But after that important hiatus, I started to write more music. I continued to vehemently disagree with what was happening, which, again, made me think of those kids in Iraq who were killed because of who they were, the music they listened to, and what they believed. While the United States didn't have death squads like Iraq, we had people of color who were being degraded and ostracized by those who had more than them. Then, in August, neo-Nazi groups descended upon Charlottesville, Virginia, and my brother Garrett went to Charlottesville to stand up to them, witnessing the horror as a white supremacist drove his car through a peaceful crowd, sending bodies into the air like pins on a lane in a bowling alley.

I wrote nine new songs for the album, including one about the events in Charlottesville, Trump's proposed ban on transgender troops in the military, adviser Stephen Miller's claims of CNN's "cosmopolitan bias," America's perceived standing in the world, and I included a remastered version of a track about Trump's comments in front of the CIA's memorial wall on his first full day in office, which I had first released in March 2016. I learned from my past mistakes, which made the recording process significantly easier. In less than two months, I recorded all nine songs, which Ben mixed and mastered in less than a week. The album was completed by Labor Day, but I decided to wait to officially release it. The day I picked was Friday the 13th.

I released my first full-length, 10-song album, which I called *In the Shadow of Tyranny*, on October 13, 2017. I designed the album cover and lyric book and sent advance copies to webzines, fanzines, blogs, and local record companies, hoping they would like the music and reach out to me. To celebrate the release, I held a party at the bar across the street from my place. Friends and family showed up, which meant a lot to me. As of the publication of this book, I had conceptualized, created, recorded, and distributed 18 original songs. As long as the internet exists, I, my family, my descendants, my friends, and anyone across the world, will be able to find and listen to Truth Assassin music. Forever. I still think back to that day in February 2012 when those tragic killings of Iraqi teenagers cut me deeply. Dozens of children were killed because of the music they listened to or the clothes they wore. Their fate introduced me to the power of music, my desire to teach music to other children, and the urge to create and distribute my own. It forever changed my life and the lives of others.

While I'm proud of my accomplishments in music, I've learned a lot of life lessons along the way:

The importance of self-awareness. Being aware of my feelings at the time I had them was crucial to understanding how my desires and goals changed over time. One thing led to the next in my musical journey, and if I hadn't recognized each of those steps, I might never have gotten to the point I did.

Pride is powerful. I am proud of all the things I have accomplished in music, and it is a healthy pride. I was proud when the U.S. Ambassador to Iraq praised me for bringing an energy to the embassy compound that, in his opinion, hadn't been there before. I was proud that I was able to get on stage and have dozens of people singing a song that I was playing. I was proud that I joined the political resistance and started Truth Assassin, exercising my First Amendment right to freedom of speech. My wife was proud of me, as were my parents, grandparents, friends, and others. Pride is powerful, and I realize that the support of others and feeling proud of what I have done is a huge motivator along my journey.

Be patient. Patience in writing music, recording music, and playing in bands is critical. Music, particularly the type of music I play, is difficult, and it's even tougher to sing and play guitar at the same time. When learning one piece of music, it is critical to learn one note or one lyric at a time. I learned that patience is also key when writing and recording music. When I made the 2017 Truth Assassin album, *In the Shadow of Tyranny*, I became frustrated when I was trying to force a song that didn't come together in the way I wanted it to. The guitar riffs didn't sound good, and the lyrics didn't fit. I recognized my frustration, took a break, and relaxed. The next day, while riding the subway to work, I started to write lyrics for a different song, and they came easily. To ensure I capitalized on the moment, I left a voicemail on my phone, sounding out the rhythm to the song, and I wrote down the chords in my journal. I returned home that night and had the entire song, including the guitars, bass, drums, and vocals recorded in two hours. If I hadn't taken a break from the song that wasn't working, I might not have so easily come up with the other song.

Perfect practice makes perfect. The more I practiced— whether it was with American Metal Conspiracy, Death Echo, or Truth Assassin—the better I got, but I realized that it wasn't just playing around for fun that made me better. A self-aware focus on doing everything exactly how it should be done, with proper form and technique, elevated my playing. The more I practiced how I wanted to lead a live show, the better I did on stage. It might have looked goofy to my bandmates, but I practiced everything I planned to do on stage. We were that much better because I had perfect practice.

Protesting is my right and my responsibility. Since I turned 18 and could vote in elections, I have voted for Republicans, Democrats, Libertarians, and Independents. I voted for George W. Bush in 2004, John McCain in 2008, Barack Obama in 2012, and Gary Johnson in 2016. I've voted for Jim Moran and George Allen, Democrats from Virginia, and George Voinovich, a Republican from Ohio. While I've been frustrated by the United States' political establishment for some time for its apparent lack of willingness to work together and cross party lines, nothing has enraged me more than what had happened since November 2016. I have never felt so emotional about a politician. But in the United States, dissent was engraved in our Constitution, and it is my right to peacefully protest. Through my music and the name Truth Assassin, I have voiced my concerns and continue to exercise my right of free speech.

Children are our future, and it is our responsibility to guide them to a future that is better than ours. One of the greatest aspects of the Sitar Arts Center is that every child who joins the center and stays in it through the age of 18 graduates from high school. In Washington, D.C., where somewhere between 60% and 70% of students graduate from high school, the Sitar Arts Center's track record is remarkable. Every day that I go to the center to teach my group of students, I think about how I'm doing my part—how little it may be—to help make these kids' lives better, give them a skill they didn't have before, give them something to look forward to each week, and help keep them off the streets and off drugs. I have come to learn that one of the most difficult things I have done in my life is teach children, and while some are model students, others lose focus easily, only practice occasionally, and have wavering motivation. Even so, I wouldn't change a thing. These kids, and any associated frustration I may have, are worth it. To quote Yogi Berra, "If I had to go back and do it all over again, I'd do it all over again." I would. I would because these children are our future, and it is our responsibility to give them as many opportunities and chances to be successful as we can.

CHAPTER 6

BECOMING "LEBANESE": MY PURSUIT OF THE ARABIC LANGUAGE

My parents sent me to Hebrew school when I was in elementary school in preparation for my bar mitzvah, but all I ever did was memorize the words, so I had no ability to comprehend any of the language or speak conversationally. I took one year of Spanish when I was in 8th grade, but the limited Spanish I knew I learned by working in restaurants in high school. I took Latin, the world's dead and unspoken language, in college and earned an A in each of my four classes. By the time I was 27 years old, I had never actually learned how to speak a foreign language.

But at that same age, I was in Baghdad, Iraq, working at the U.S. Embassy, and I saw an advertisement in the embassy's newsletter about free Arabic language classes. I only had a few months left in my year-long assignment, but I thought it would be a fun thing to do before I left, so I enrolled and attended an Arabic class one hour per week. In those few classes I had, I found that I really enjoyed learning about the language and liked to study it in my spare time. Even better, the instructor praised my pronunciation and accent. Maybe I had something here.

After I returned home from Iraq, I asked management if they would support me attending full-time Arabic language training, as it seemed at the time that most U.S. government agencies that dealt with foreign affairs needed Arabic speakers. I felt I had a clear knack for the language, and I thought that should be supported.

"No, we need you here at your desk, not out in language training," they told me. My request was denied.

I persisted, and management caved, albeit only a little. Instead of full-time Arabic language training, I was allocated funding for six hours per week—two hours a day, three days per week—for six months. It was better than nothing, I thought, and maybe I could make something of it.

My strategic goal was to pass the State Department's Arabic language test. The year I spent in Baghdad was a phenomenal experience, but I only had the opportunity to serve there because the embassy needed extra people and I volunteered. I wanted to make it a lifelong career.

I had already passed the Oral Assessment, the final test to be placed on the register, the list of applicants who passed every test in the process and were waiting for a slot in a training class. The State Department was in dire need of Arabic speakers to work in embassies and consulates across the Middle East, so if I passed the Arabic language test, my score from the final test would receive a bonus, and I'd have a shorter wait on the register. After I completed the training, the State Department could assign me to a consular section to conduct personal interviews with foreigners seeking visas to enter the United States. While I wouldn't need to have heated debates on political issues, I had to easily converse with applicants, in their own language, about their daily affairs, families, jobs, income levels, and more. That was my goal.

The problem was that Arabic is an extremely difficult language to learn. It has more letters than English, and its letters also change forms if they appear in the beginning, middle, or end of a word. There are vowel accents, dots, and guttural stops. The verbs appear at the beginning of the sentence, and the subject appears at some point later in the sentence, if at all. I knew from talking with friends that the State Department's language test was conducted over the phone with two graders who asked a variety of questions on numerous topics. While the test was graded pass/fail, I learned that to pass the test, I would need to be able to talk about simple daily affairs in the past, present, and future, as well as world events, politics, and the news.

It took most students a full year of dedicated studying to get to that level. Usually, full-time language training consisted of students learning in a classroom for five hours a day, five days a week. Students studied at home for three to four hours per night, as well as additional time studying on weekends. In total, a full-time language student had about 1,200 hours of classroom time and 1,000 hours of studying at home per year—a total of 2,200 hours. And for some people I knew, even that wasn't enough.

I had six hours of class time per week, plus my own studying at home, so I wouldn't have anywhere near that amount of training. By the end of six months, I would total about 150 hours of classroom time and, at most, about 200 hours studying on my own. I had 10% of the time to do 100% of the work. Could I do it? Time, and the amount of effort I put in, would tell.

On the day of my first lesson, I was assigned a dedicated Arabic instructor. Her name was Fadwa. She was a short, dark-haired woman in her fifties who was born and raised in Damascus, Syria. She told me she had become an American citizen many years before and loved to travel back to Syria, telling me how wonderful a place it was before the civil war started in 2012. In our first class, Fadwa asked me what I hoped to accomplish from the class.

"Passing the Arabic language test with State," I said.

Fadwa nodded her head slightly. "If you work hard," she said, "inshallah."

I learned "inshallah" when I was in Iraq. Its literal meaning is "by the will of God" or "God willing," and on the surface, her comment could be taken as a vote of confidence. But, as I also learned, the word has a second meaning, which comes from an idiom about Arab culture:

How does an Arab say yes? He says "na'am." (The literal translation for "yes" in the language.) How does an Arab say no? He says inshallah.

My intuition told me that Fadwa didn't think I could do it, so I felt even more determined. I wanted to prove to her how much I could learn. As our first class continued, Fadwa taught me some prepositional words in Arabic, simple things like: on, under, beside, and near. Eight words total. Eight words should be simple. Except they weren't. I was struggling mightily. I sat in class for an hour trying to pummel these eight words into my brain, but it didn't seem to be working. At home later that evening, I made flashcards for each new word. Card after card, I tried to memorize the words. After almost two hours, I finally felt like I had learned them, but I was exhausted. In that moment, I had a realization: This is much more difficult than I thought. How can I do this? If it takes me almost three hours to learn eight simple words, how am I going to learn the rest of the language?

I calmed down. "One day at a time, one class at a time, one word at a time," I told myself.

One of the best things about the language school I attended is that each new student prepaid for the first two weeks of class, and that payment was non-refundable. Even though I was embarrassed that I could barely learn eight words and my motivation had waned, I was financially committed.

Two days later, I returned to class and Fadwa threw more words, phrases, and constructions at me. It was too much. It was like she was giving me all this information, knowing I couldn't handle it. In that moment, I thought of a passage I read in the book *The Tao of Daily Life,* which tells the story of a goat at the bottom of a well. Nobody wanted the goat, so the townspeople threw trash into the well on top of the goat, hoping to keep him there. Instead of losing hope, the goat used each piece of trash to climb higher and higher until he was able to escape and run free. Instead of seeing the words that Fadwa threw at me as pieces of trash to keep me down, I would see each word as a stepping stone to get to the top of the well. I had a goal, and I was going to get after it. A journey of a thousand miles starts with a single step, and in my case, a single word. One step at a time. One word at a time.

As my classes progressed through January, I got better, and I had learned pronouns, basic verbs, and numbers. I was starting to have a better overall understanding of the language. I studied every night and on weekends, and with each class and study session, the language was becoming easier to learn. I felt like I was entering a groove, and I didn't want anything to get in my way.

"Hey, Parker, we're going to watch football on Sunday. Wanna come?" a friend would ask.

"Nah, I gotta study." Back to the books.

In February and March, I found my rhythm. I arrived at class 15 minutes early to go over my notes and homework from the previous class, focusing my mind on my new language. Fadwa and I would fly through the next two hours, practicing, learning, speaking, and reading. When I got home, I'd study more. I was putting full sentences together and was able to memorize about 20 words per day. Maybe I did have a knack for this language.

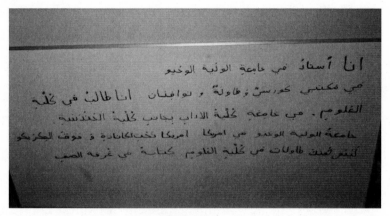

A picture of the whiteboard I used to practice my Arabic writing.

One day in class, one of Fadwa's former students knocked on the door, and they spoke for a few minutes. I listened to their conversation in Arabic and was impressed that the girl could speak so quickly, but something jumped out at me: she sounded entirely American. It was like she knew every Arabic word in the dictionary but didn't *sound* like she did.

"She is a very good Arabic speaker, Parker," Fadwa said to me. "Do you agree?"

"She clearly knows the language, but I don't think she has a very good accent," I said.

"Parker, you have a great accent." Fadwa told me. "It's not something many people can do. You sound like me, a Syrian or

Lebanese. I think you might have Middle Eastern in your heritage." I was proud knowing that a native Arab thought I had a good accent, and although I didn't know much of the language, at least I could speak what I did know very well.

While I had a good accent and had made a lot of progress, I was concerned that I wasn't moving fast enough. It was already April, and I wasn't able to talk about the politics and news I needed. I realized that my limited time in class restricted my growth and that I needed more ways to get more Arabic in my brain for longer periods of time.

While I read and spoke a lot on my own, particularly at home, I realized that I needed to practice more conversations, so I used my personal network to have meetups with other Arabic speakers, particularly ones who were better than me. They spoke to me with new words, phrases, and grammatical constructions, and I took notes on what was said so I could try to incorporate them into my own vocabulary and dialogue. To further aid my listening comprehension, Fadwa gave me a book of Arabic CDs that I could listen to in my car. As much as I loved music, I listened to those CDs incessantly in April and May.

As May came to an end, I could speak in Arabic about things in the past, present, and future, and I could describe my surroundings, how I got to class, and my family, education, background, military service, and more. I was making a lot of progress, and it felt good. Could I pass the test? I didn't know, but I knew I was getting closer each day.

As I walked into class in the beginning of June, I had exactly 28 days until my language test, and it was time to devote every possible moment to my training. I joined another Arabic speaking group, listened to Arabic videos on YouTube, and started reading news on

Arabic websites. While I couldn't translate the articles word for word, I could piece them together and found that I could understand the main points of the articles. I wasn't perfect, but I didn't need to be, I just needed to understand the gist of them as best I could. I learned that speaking another language was not about speaking it perfectly all the time, but speaking it well enough that someone understood my point and I understood theirs. In a few weeks, I would need to understand the testers and needed them to understand me.

In the middle of June, I received extra funding to attend full-time language training for the remaining two weeks before my test. For those two weeks, I'd be like any other language student: five hours a day, five days a week, with several more hours of studying at night. Fadwa and I hit it hard, as hard as we could, and on my second-to-last day, Fadwa asked Leila, another Arabic instructor, to join our class and give me a mock test.

Leila was tall and thin with flowing black hair and olive skin, all of which I attributed to her Lebanese ancestry. She sat across from me and asked me questions, and she and Fadwa listened to my responses. I incorporated complex language where I could, showing how much I had learned and grown. I was putting Fadwa's advice to work: "If you don't show it, they won't know it."

"Parker, I'm very impressed," Leila told me in English at the end of our 10-minute, Arabic-only conversation. "I'm not going to say whether you will pass the test or not, but I will say that I'm amazed that you could come this far in only six months of part-time classroom learning."

I smiled. "Shukran jazeelan," I told her. ("Thank you very much," in Arabic.) I was proud of my effort up to this point, as was

Fadwa. It was a testament to her, as well, for how far I had come. She enabled me to succeed.

Class ended on Friday, June 21, and I studied on my own through the weekend and into the following week, taking a short respite to celebrate my birthday on June 26, two days before my test. What a birthday present it would be, I thought to myself, if I passed the test. It would be incredible. What a feat! What a journey! Never stopping. Never quitting. Never giving up. A real-life example of getting after it.

The next thing I knew it was June 28, 2013, at 2:30 in the afternoon. This was it. Everything I worked toward for the past six months came down to this moment. I focused my mind and sat at my bar-height table in my living room. I plugged my earphones into my mobile phone and dialed the number of the testing center. When prompted, I entered my special code into the phone system and was connected through to the testers.

"Hello. Are we speaking with Parker Schaffel?"

"Na'am! Ismee Parker Schaffel! Kaif al-hahl?" I responded in Arabic. (Yes. My name is Parker Schaffel. How are you?)

"Parker, the test has not begun yet, we'll speak in English until the test begins," a tester responded. "There are two of us on the line, and we will both be asking you questions and listening to your answers." They told me to use as much different vocabulary I could to demonstrate my mastery of the language. "If you don't show it, we won't know it," they said, an eerie, but appropriate echo of what Fadwa had told me a few weeks before.

The test began with simple questions about my day, my education, and background, and I felt confident about my answers. As the questions became more difficult, I closed my eyes and tried to key in on words I knew, while not getting hung up on ones I didn't. From what I could tell, they wanted to know about certain geopolitical situations and events in international affairs. My mind raced and shifted back and forth between Arabic and English as I cobbled together sentences in my head. I answered as best I could, in as much detail as possible. I just hoped it was good enough. "Parker, in a few days, you'll receive an email with the grade of your test, which will only be reported as pass/fail," one of the instructors said at the end of the call. I had done everything I could. At this point, hope was all I had left, and I wouldn't give it up until the end. I stayed positive and waited for the test score.

The night after the test and through the weekend, I relaxed and let my brain rest—the first time I felt like I had done so since I started language training six months before. As a U.S. Navy reservist, I had received orders to report in late July to Manama, Bahrain, the home of the U.S. Navy's Naval Central Forces Command, so I took the following week off work to prepare for my assignment.

The next day, Tuesday, July 2, as I was driving to visit my parents, my phone beeped. At the next red light, about two blocks from my parents' condo, I looked at my phone and saw I had an email from the State Department testing center. With the light still red, I tapped the email, opened it up, and read.

Mr. Schaffel,

You did not pass the BEX Arabic (Formal Standard) language test on 6/28/2013. This test was administered on a pass/fail basis, no other grade is provided. You may retest again in six months.

There it was. It was the email I was waiting for, but it had the information I didn't want to see. I failed. I put the phone back down and drove the remaining two blocks, parked my car, and looked at my phone again.

"Did not pass."

I was amused at the positive language used to describe what really happened. I failed. My failure meant that my score on the register would not get the foreign language bonus. I knew, deep down, that my score, without any bonuses, wasn't good enough to get me into a training class. I needed the language bonus, but I didn't get it. I did everything I could, studied as hard as I could, listened to every CD I could, but it just didn't work out as I wanted it to. And while I was proud of what I had accomplished and thought about the praise that Fadwa and the other Arabic instructor at my school had given me, in the end, pride and a test failure were all I had. I was disappointed. I was upset. I was mad. But I also knew that I did my best and I had no regrets. I did everything I could.

A few weeks later, I flew to Bahrain for my U.S. Navy Reserve assignment. As I got to know more of the other officers stationed there, I met an officer named James with whom I shared a love for rugby. "I love playing, but my back is messed up," he said. "I herniated a disc a few games ago, but luckily we have the nice hospital close to the base and I go there for physical therapy."

Intrigued, I told James about some lingering tendonitis issues I had in my foot, and he recommended I go to the hospital to see his physical therapist. I had never been to a Middle Eastern hospital before, but I was willing to give it a try. I rode a bicycle to the hospital, which was about a five-minute ride from where I was living off base. When I showed up for my appointment, I was introduced to my physical therapist.

"Hello, my name is Jamil," he said as he stuck out his hand. I returned the handshake and introduced myself. "Please follow me," he said, motioning us back to the exam room. As we walked, Jamil told me that he was Jordanian, had been a physical therapist for almost 30 years, and had been living in Bahrain for the last 20. He was older, bald, in his late fifties, and spoke softly. I felt welcomed and safe, so I told him that I had just arrived in Bahrain, was living at a local hotel, and was working at the Navy base.

As we sat down in the exam room, Jamil asked me to take off my shoe and sock and to describe the pain in my foot from the tendonitis. Jamil obviously spoke Arabic, so I decided I would try to speak to him in his native language. After all, I spent all that time learning Arabic, and there I was in an Arab country.

"Laysa 'alm fee q'dmee, alan, leken qublah yomain, 'alm katheeran," I said, telling Jamil, in Arabic, that I didn't have any pain in my foot at that moment, but that I had a lot of pain two days ago.

He looked up at me, furrowed his brow, and spoke in English: "What did you just say?" I repeated what I said in Arabic.

"Anta tetekellum al-lugah al-arabiyah?!" (You speak the Arabic language?!) Jamil broke out in a smile and became very animated, bringing his hands up to his head in seeming disbelief. I grinned and nodded. I continued speaking Arabic, telling Jamil that I had studied for six months before coming to Bahrain and that, while I had a lot more to learn, I was happy with what I had learned in that short time. "You are only the third American I've ever known to speak Arabic," he said in Arabic. It felt really good to know that I could impress Jamil by speaking in his own language.

I returned a few days later for my next appointment and walked into Jamil's exam room, passing another Arab-looking man on my way. I greeted Jamil, sat on the table, and we started speaking in Arabic, as we had done the appointment before. The curtain to our room had a slight crack and I noticed that the same man I saw from earlier passed our room, looking at me for a few seconds. Strange, I thought. I continued talking with Jamil in Arabic until he asked me to go into the exercise room to begin strength training exercises. Usually Jamil was right behind me, but this time he was gone, only appearing after about a minute. Jamil walked up to me and spoke to me in English.

"I just had a man walk up to me and ask who you were and why you were here in the hospital," he said. I furrowed my brow, looking puzzled. "He asked why there was a Lebanese man in a hospital in Bahrain. I told him that you were an American and weren't from Lebanon. He said, 'That man is not American. I saw him and heard him speak Arabic. He's Lebanese!'"

My puzzled expression quickly transitioned to a wide grin. Sure, I hadn't passed the phone test, but in this moment it didn't matter. I spoke Arabic well enough, with a good accent, that another Arab thought I was an Arab. There was no test that could assess that. That was left up to a stranger in Bahrain, who would forever remind me that, while tests mattered, real life mattered more. I could rest knowing that I had passed the true test: speaking a foreign language in another country and passing for a native speaker.

I learned a lot of lessons along the way, things that remain important to me today.

Break down long-term goals into the smallest pieces possible. While the task seemed daunting in the beginning, it became much more palatable when I broke it down into smaller pieces. One day at a time, one lesson at a time, one word at a time, and sometimes one letter at a time. My thousand-mile journey began with a single step, and it is made up of thousands of those single steps along the way. My learning was exactly that—one step at a time, over and over and over again, on a six-month journey.

Sometimes short-term sacrifice is necessary to accomplish a long-term goal. While difficult, I knew that I had to make short-term sacrifices to achieve long-term gains. I didn't spend a lot of time with friends, I didn't date any girls (I hadn't yet met my wife), and I didn't do much else on weekends other than study. For that six-month period, I worked, exercised, and studied. I'm confident that if I didn't study as hard as I did, I never would have been a successful conversational Arabic speaker and my efforts would have been for naught.

Recognize your strengths and concentrate on them. It was clear to me that I had a knack for the language, and that provided a lot of motivation to keep going. If I had been studying, perhaps, another language or another subject in which I did not have an innate ability, I would not have been as successful. I realized how important it was to ensure that my efforts are put toward things I'm passionate about, so my preparation and training will be easier and more effective.

Ask for everything you want, and you could be surprised at what you get. Asking for a lot and negotiating for less got me the training I wanted, albeit not all of it, but enough. If I had asked for a few hours of training per week, I might have gotten nothing, but I asked for full-time training and got six-hours per week, and that class time, along with my intense self-study, got me the recognition I received in Bahrain.

Doors will close, but windows will open. Failing the test was a major setback in my journey, but it also opened other windows for future opportunities. If I had passed the exam and earned a spot, I wouldn't have written this story and this book, I wouldn't have married the wonderful woman I did, I wouldn't have had the time to start a solo music project, I wouldn't be teaching inner-city children how to play guitar, and I wouldn't have had the time to do the other things I've done since 2013.

I was "Lebanese." When I returned from Bahrain, I intended to continue studying and learning Arabic, but my office told me that they would not provide any additional funding, and the private instruction was too expensive to pay on my own. In 2014, when I reached my 18-month time limit on the register, my name was removed, and I was told I could apply again but that I would have to restart the entire process. Although I decided not to pursue it any further and rebrand myself as a strategic communications professional, I'll never forget that day in Bahrain when I was "Lebanese."

CHAPTER 7

FINDING MY FIT: MY NINE-YEAR JOURNEY TO THE RIGHT PLACE IN THE CIA

"Workplace culture is changing," said Preston Peterson, the facilitator for my group's offsite in November 2008. "Baby boomers are in the highest ranks, and they are leading millennials who are just joining the workforce. The gap between them is wide, which is why we need to discuss it to help bridge that gap."

I was a 23-year-old millennial myself, and I agreed with Preston's point. But it didn't seem like anyone else did. They were dead silent. *There's dozens of people here,* I thought to myself. *How come no one is saying anything?* I had just returned from Afghanistan a few weeks before and was eager to get involved in my office, so I spoke up.

"I think one of the most important things to consider is the underlying reason why different generations took the jobs they did," I said. "Many baby boomers were just happy to get a job when they started out in the 1970s, while for us millennials, the job market is better and more diverse, and we have a desire to be a part of global change." Preston nodded as I spoke and told the group that he agreed with my points, providing some additional data and context.

I added a few more thoughts to the discussion, and for the rest of the module it seemed like we were the only two engaged. What impressed me most about Preston was his incredible ability to command a room. He beamed with confidence and energy, and he always seemed to know the right question to ask or the right thing to say. I hadn't met anyone like him before, but I knew I wanted to get to know him better. Much to my surprise, Preston came up to me after the session.

"Thanks for starting off that conversation," he told me. "It was like crickets in there until you made some really great points." I thanked Preston for his compliment, but I didn't think I had done or said anything mind-blowing. At the same time, I recognized that it was one of the first meaningful compliments I'd received at the CIA in the year and four months since I started my career as a military intelligence analyst.

When I returned to work after the offsite, I immediately researched and signed up for two leadership courses taught by Preston: one in March 2009 for "rising leaders," and another in August 2009 based on the leadership and self-development book *The Seven Habits of Highly Effective People* by Stephen Covey. As 2009 rolled in, I did the best I could in my analytic job, but under the surface I counted the days until I could take the first course with Preston. After the first two-day course was over, I went back to my job and again found myself waiting until August. Spring turned to summer, and I spent three memorable days with Preston during his *Seven Habits* course, in which he walked us through modules of self-reflection, teamwork, values building, and motivating teams. I had a fantastic time and learned an enormous amount about myself. Before I knew it, the three days were up. I had to go back to my analytic job. But I didn't want to be there. I wanted to be back in the class. I wanted to be working with Preston.

The problem, as I determined, was that I just wasn't a good analyst. I joined the Agency in 2007 as a military analyst, but I wasn't motivated and I knew that I was only mediocre on my best day. My colleagues wrote papers with better arguments and deeper strategic analysis than me, and they completed them in less time. It was a tough realization, but it was true. I just wasn't cut out to be an analyst.

Within a week of returning to my office after the *Seven Habits* course, I felt like I found my true calling at the CIA: working with Preston and his team, the Professional Development Group, so I emailed him to tell him exactly that. I wrote about how much I enjoyed his classes, how I was already applying lessons I learned from the classes in my life, and I stated my intention to work with him. "If you ever need an assistant or an apprentice of any kind, let me know and I'll come running," I wrote. Preston responded later that day and told me that it would be great to have me on his team, but there weren't any open positions at the time. He said he would keep an eye out for vacancies on his team.

I had no idea how long it would take me to get to Preston's group, but I was determined. I knew there was bureaucracy, red tape, and that timing would play a huge factor, so I reached out to a mentor, Deb, to seek her advice. She was a manager in another analytic group and a person with whom I had an instant connection because we had both graduated from Ohio State. When we met, I told her about my intention to leave analysis and join the Professional Development Group.

"Before you run out on analysis, you should try another analytic team," Deb said. "Because maybe it's the team you're on and the issues you're working. You might enjoy it more if you were on a different team."

I didn't really want to, but with no openings on Preston's team, I took Deb's advice. She introduced me to Rick, a team chief in her group. I liked the guy, and the issues on his team seemed interesting enough that I applied to an open position on his team in October 2009. Within a week of starting, Rick was promoted to be Deb's deputy, which meant my new team and I would get a new team chief.

Just great, I thought. Half the reason I joined the team was because people spoke highly of Rick.

A few weeks later, the excitement I had from the job change faded. On a normal day in early December, I wrote a joint analytic paper with my teammate Natalie, and we received a lot of pushback and clarifying questions from Rey, our new team chief, and several other senior managers, far more than normal. It was hour upon hour of back and forth, and by the end of it, now the early evening, I felt like I couldn't think anymore. My brain was fried. I knew plenty of analysts whose energy increased from those types of debates, but not me. I just wanted to go home, and I didn't even care what the paper said anymore.

When the back-and-forth debate ended with an approved draft, I finally left work around seven o'clock at night. I was tired and angry, so angry that this type of work had taken such a toll on me. I was 25 years old, and I was supposed to feel young, strong, and healthy. Instead, I felt weak, helpless, and confused. As I drove home, I cranked up the volume on my car radio and sang along to any song I knew. All the anger and emotion I had from that day was flowing out of me through the music; it was cathartic. I was getting close to home, with only three more traffic lights to go. Then it happened.

BANG! As I drove through an intersection, a car turned in front of me, crossing my path from left to right. I hit the brakes and tried to swerve as my anti-lock braking system pumped the brake fluid into my calipers, jerking my car to a halt. But it was too late. My Honda Accord had crashed into a Jeep Grand Cherokee.

I collected myself and got out of my car. I saw a woman step out of the Jeep. She seemed shaken, but uninjured. "Are you okay?" I asked.

"Yes, I'm fine," she responded. "You?"

"Yes, I'm alright. Thanks."

The damage to our vehicles didn't appear as bad as I initially thought, and we were able to drive the cars out of the intersection onto the shoulder. The Fairfax County police officer who arrived on the scene cited me for causing the collision because the Jeep had the right of way. But that was crazy to me. I thought I was the one with a green light, because if I didn't have one, I obviously wouldn't have gone through the intersection. But then I realized what happened. The set of traffic lights for the intersection I was crossing appeared almost in alignment with the next set of lights for the next intersection. The green lights I saw were for the next intersection; my lights were red. Like the officer said, the collision was my fault.

I was barely able to get the car the final mile home before it died in the parking lot of my housing complex. The damage to the engine compartment must have been worse than I initially thought. Still sitting in the driver's seat, I began to bawl. It shouldn't be like this. I had had enough with analysis. Two years of trying and this is what I had become. A 25-year-old man who had been overtaken by an analytic paper. I couldn't do it anymore. I wouldn't do it anymore. The events of that day led me into a dangerous situation, and I decided in that moment that I wasn't going to let it happen again. I decided that terrible December evening would be the final cataclysm of my analytic career. It was time to push even harder to get out of analysis and find a way to work with Preston and his team.

The next day, I called Deb, told her what happened and that I was going to take the day off. When I returned to work the following day, I met with Deb and Rick. "I can't do it anymore," I said. "What happened two days ago pushed me over the edge. I'm done with analysis."

"Parker, I know you're upset," Deb replied.

"Deb, I could have killed someone!" I yelled, cutting her off. I was making my stand. "Don't you get that? It's not just that I'm upset. What if there was a baby in the backseat of that Jeep? I couldn't think that night all because of this job!" I made my case, while being respectful, articulate, and passionate. I told them how I had tried analysis for long enough and it wasn't working for me. I wanted to work with Preston.

"It's just not that easy to switch into something else," Deb said. "Any other position outside of analysis would be a rotation, and that would need to be approved." Deb was talking about one of the human resources processes at the CIA, in which each person was owned by what the Agency called career services, a cohort of employees that all did the same type of work. CIA, like other Fortune 500 companies, is made up of hundreds of career paths, and if I wanted to work in a job outside my career service, my career service board would have to approve it. In my case, approval would come from the analytic career service board. The conversation ended with no definitive way forward, other than me going back to my desk.

In January 2010, I received an email asking if anyone in my office was interested in working a six-month assignment in the CIA's Operations Center. I knew other analysts who had worked there, and it seemed better than what I was currently doing, especially because it would get me out of analysis for six months and afford me time to figure out more paths to get to Preston's team. Because my office was required to provide a body to the Operations Center, I volunteered and my name was sent forward. I started two months later.

Despite making connections in other offices and meeting with other managers and mentors, the six months came and went with no clear way ahead. I returned to my analytic job in October 2010, meeting with Deb on my first day back in the office. "Parker, we're glad to have you back and get you writing again," Deb told me. "We want you to keep up the good work."

Keep up the good work? What was she talking about? I had always tried hard, but my work was never that good. No one came to me saying, "We have this strategic issue and we want you, Parker, to handle it."

I left her office, went back to my desk, and emailed Preston, asking for advice. "Did you read the book *The Four Agreements* I told you about?" he responded, referring to a book written by Don Miguel Ruiz.

"Of course. I found it fascinating," I responded. "I'm already trying to incorporate some of the lessons from the book into my personal life."

"What do you think about helping me develop a leadership course based on lessons from the book?" Preston wanted me to work on a leadership course with him? Was he kidding? There was no question about it! I was thrilled at the offer to collaborate. It might not have been a position on his team, but it was the next best thing.

We met up the following week and worked on the course for about a month, coordinating through emails and phone calls to talk about how the book's lessons should be incorporated into an educational lesson on personal and professional leadership. At the end of the month, we had our finished product: *The Four Agreements*, a two-hour seminar as part of Preston's leadership seminar series he called *Leadership Now!* Building the course with him was a great experience, and I felt grateful and humbled to produce something that was still being taught at the CIA nine years after we created it.

From 2011 to 2013, I worked in a few different positions in the government and military, including working for the State Department at the U.S. Embassy in Iraq and my deployment to the Middle East with the U.S. Navy. In 2014, with no other place to go after my deployment, I resigned from the State Department, rejoined the CIA, and returned to analysis.

A few months later, a friend of mine who knew I wanted to get out of analysis wrote me a one-line email: "What do you think?" Attached at the bottom was a link to a job vacancy to run the CIA's internal news platform in the Office of Public Affairs (OPA). On the surface, it seemed like a good fit. I'd be able to write interesting stories about things going on at the Agency, as well as learn about strategic communications, content strategy, photography, and more. Preston still didn't have an opening on his team, so I decided to pursue this position in the meantime. But just like four years before when I had the accident, the new position wasn't part of the analytic career service, which meant I needed approval even to apply. I spoke with Joe, who was the chief of the team and a guy I had known for a few years. We had worked on the same team in the past, and I knew he didn't care for me.

"Do you think this is it?" he asked me in a point-blank manner. While it seemed like a strange question, my intuition knew his underlying premise: he didn't want to deal with me anymore. I didn't produce much analysis, and he knew my motivation and confidence were low. He didn't want me there. I didn't want to be there.

"Yes, this is it," I assured him. He routed the request up the management chain, and I waited for an answer. I don't know what made this position different than the other times I tried to make a switch, but for whatever reason, they approved it. I applied, was offered the job, and started in April 2014.

The new position, officially listed as an editor in OPA, was part of a career service called Executive Staff Officers (ESOs), a hodge-podge of employees who performed staff work in the offices of Public Affairs, Congressional Affairs, Military Affairs, the Operations Center, and a few others. In addition to those offices, a few ESOs filled positions in other CIA offices, and I knew that Preston's office had one or two. If I could do a good job in public affairs and become an ESO, I would substantially increase my chances of getting an assignment on Preston's team.

As 2014 came to a close, two important things happened. First, Preston told me that he and his teammates were planning for January 2015 a day-long *Leadership Now!* course, which consisted of presentations, group discussions, and self-awareness activities, as well as a wrap-up event of back-to-back presentations on leadership topics by members of the workforce. The three representatives would come from the three groups of Agency employees: the Senior Intelligence Service (SIS), supervisors, and non-supervisors, the latter of which would be selected through an application process. "You should definitely apply," Preston told me. "Betsy wants you to apply, as well," he added, referring to his team chief in the Professional Development Group.

"No question about it," I told him. Excited for the opportunity to work with Preston again, I went home that night and developed a 10-minute presentation focusing on my view of the difference between leadership and management. I used personal experiences—lessons I learned from the military, public and private sector, and leadership books I had read.

I submitted my proposal the next day, and a week later I found out that I was the non-supervisor who would be speaking at this seminar. I was extremely excited. It was my first real opportunity to get in front of CIA colleagues and share my thoughts, give them energy, and motivate them. I prepared relentlessly because this was my time to shine.

On the day of the class, I arrived about 20 minutes early, said hello to Preston, and took my seat on stage. My nerves grew as I awaited the SIS officer and the supervisor to finish their discussions. Then it was my turn. I took a breath and rose from my chair, standing in front of the 100 people in the room.

"How many people here think there is a difference between management and leadership?" I asked. About three-quarters of the attendees raised their hands.

"And of those with your hands raised, how many can define that difference?" Most hands went down.

"So, is leadership like love? You can't define it, but you know it when you feel it?" Most of the attendees smiled, and some laughed. I began to relax and find my groove.

"To me, management is the process of planning, organizing, coordinating, directing, and controlling," I said, referring to lessons I learned my junior year of Air Force ROTC. "Leadership, on the other hand, is the art of ensuring people have the motivation, preparation, and confidence to do their jobs," recalling the lessons I learned from football, skydiving, and the military.

Attendees nodded their heads. I told them how I developed these philosophies, shared how they impacted my life, and provided examples of how we could use these principles in the workplace. When I finished, I received a round of applause and had several people at the event, including Preston, tell me how much they enjoyed my presentation. I was proud that I could do something that resonated with so many people, especially my dear friend Preston.

When I returned to work the next day, I walked by a woman in the hallway who stopped me. "I was at the *Leadership Now!* event yesterday, and I just wanted to say how much I enjoyed your presentation," she said. Humbled, I thanked her for her compliment and told her to keep in touch if she ever needed anything.

A few days later, Chris, Preston's second-level supervisor, the chief of the Professional Development Group, sent my management team in OPA an email about how inspiring my presentation was. I thrived on feedback, and it was great to know that my 10-minute presentation was so appreciated by others. I didn't need more motivation to join the Professional Development Group, but this provided more, and having the support of the group chief was especially welcome.

The second important thing that happened in early 2015 was an opening of the application process to officers to apply to convert to the ESO career service. It was my chance to get out of the stranglehold of analysis and have more control of my own destiny. All I had to do was meet the minimum criteria, have a successful application, and rock an interview. The selection board would have no choice but to convert me. If I was successful, I'd be one step closer to joining Preston's team.

But as red tape had hampered me before, red tape hampered me again. "Applicants must have 12 *consecutive* months working in an ESO office," the requirements indicated. I didn't have 12 consecutive months; I had only been in OPA for 10 months. Even so, I had worked in the Operations Center for more than six months and the Office of Military Affairs for a shorter stint when I served in Afghanistan. Both of those were ESO offices, giving me 19 months of *cumulative* experience across three ESO offices. I knew the requirement said consecutive, but surely 19 months in three offices was more appealing than 12 months in one office. I submitted my application and sent it in, noting my situation.

"I'm sorry, Parker," the human resources manager responded. "We have discussed this and have denied your application. The requirement is 12 *consecutive* months, as it is written in the policy."

I was pissed. Seriously? They were prioritizing someone with 12 months in one office over someone with 19 months in three offices? I felt I clearly brought more to the table than most other applicants, and the only reason I couldn't apply was because of a technicality in the policy. Despite my pleas, they didn't budge. My application was denied. The analytic career service board still owned me. I would have to wait for the next call for ESO applications, and I had no idea when that would be.

Timing was not on my side, especially several months later, in October 2015, when I read the contents of an email from Betsy, Preston's boss. "Parker, we just posted a vacancy to be Preston's deputy. Please apply." Seriously? Was it finally happening? The position was vacant, and they were seeking *my* application for it? It was incredible. My dream position was finally available, and the group's management wanted me in it. I jumped out of my chair and immediately ran into my boss's office, trying to play it cool.

"Hey, Stacey, I just wanted to let you know I got an email about a vacancy to work with Preston," I said. "I know I haven't filled this job for two years, as is the norm, but as you know, this is something I've wanted to do for a long while."

She took a deep breath and spoke softly. "I know that you've been trying to find your way in this organization for a long time," she said. "And I know that working on Preston's team is something that has always been important to you. Let me talk with the folks upstairs," she said, referring to the director and deputy director of OPA. I thanked her and went back to my desk, thinking everything might finally be falling into place. The fact that she would even ask made me feel like I finally had someone who understood me and appreciated where I wanted to go. Stacey's support meant a lot.

A few days later, she told me that OPA management agreed that the Professional Development Group was the best place for me, even though my departure would put our team down an officer in the short term. Stacey was placing my interests before her own, and I was very appreciative of that. While I was still technically owned by the analysis office, I didn't think my application to Preston's team would matter as the analysis career service board had already approved my assignment to OPA. I was already out of the office, so what was it to them? I submitted my application, interviewed with Preston and a few other managers in the group, and waited. About two weeks later, unsurprisingly, Preston and his team selected me for the position and started working the transfer process through human resources.

I was excited, and everything seemed to be going smoothly, until I received an instant message from a guy named Eric, a deputy group chief in my old analytic office. "Parker, I saw that you applied to another position. We'd like to meet with you to discuss your plans. Please let me know when you're available tomorrow."

"My plan is very simple," I typed. "I'm going to work in the Professional Development Group, and I need you to approve it in the system." His request for a meeting seemed silly to me. I was already out of his office, so I was just a name on a paper. My current managers, the ones who would be shorthanded without me, supported my move, so why did it matter to Eric? Nevertheless, he persisted, so I agreed to meet him at 2:30 in the afternoon the next day.

When I walked into Eric's office, he was sitting down with two of his colleagues: a guy named Bob and a woman named Susan. Bob had taken over for Joe as the team chief of my old team, but I never worked for him. I didn't know Susan and had never met her before. I sat down across from them, Bob to my left, Eric in front of me, and Susan to my right. My back was literally against the wall in Eric's office.

The three of them exchanged glances for a few seconds until Susan spoke, breaking the silence. "Parker, we have denied your application to the Professional Development Group."

What? My mind started racing. This must be a joke. She must be kidding. But she can't be joking because jokes are made amongst friends, and I wasn't friends with these people. None of them are laughing. No one is smiling. There's no "gotcha!" She was serious. I smirked, started to shake my head back and forth, and looked at the ground. She spoke again.

"We are short on military analysts, so we can't approve you or anyone going on back-to-back assignments outside the office. The only way that this assignment can happen is if you're not part of the analytic career service."

This seemed crazy to me. "I tried earlier this year," I said. "But I wasn't allowed because of the policy."

"Well, that may be the case, but we still stand by our position."

I couldn't believe it. They *seriously* wanted me to return to the office to be an analyst again. Were they on drugs? I wasn't a good analyst. I never provided anything of value in that job. These people cared nothing for me or my future. They just wanted a warm body in a desk chair. As I processed all of this, Susan broke the silence again, saying something that stupefied me, still giving me chills to this day: "Parker, we think it's in your best interest to return to analysis."

What. The. ****.

What?? My best interest? How do *you* know what *my* best interest is? I had never worked for any of these people before, and somehow, someway, they knew my best interest better than I knew my own. They weren't my parents, mentors, advisers, or confidants. The only relation we had was the fact that I reported to them administratively. I looked at each of them, one at a time and spoke calmly and softly: "I will quit this organization before I return to analysis."

I was seething, and they knew it. Before I did or said anything I would regret, I stood up and left the room. I went back to my office, told Stacey about the meeting, and said I needed to take the rest of the day off. She understood, and I went home. The next day I appealed the situation to the human resources department and was told the only option I had was to join the ESO career service, something I had tried before but was snubbed by the system. Another day.

Another roadblock. But I wouldn't give up. I would stay positive. I would make it happen. I continued my work as an editor in OPA.

As 2015 was coming to an end, I received the announcement I had been waiting for: the next call for applications to join the ESO career service. This was finally it. This was my time. I'd been in the Office of Public Affairs for 18 consecutive months and wouldn't be stymied by the 12-month consecutive requirement. Nothing could stop me now. I opened the application packet and started to read.

"Applicants must have at least 12 *cumulative* months supporting ESO offices." *Cumulative*. I laughed. Of course. They changed the policy. If only it had been this way the last time, I would have been in my dream job at this point. But I also knew that I could spend all day living in the world of "if onlys" and "what ifs" that wouldn't get me anywhere. I couldn't change the past, and the future would bring what it would. The only solace I had at the time was the possibility that my appeal earlier in the year was the catalyst that sparked the policy change. Perhaps I helped pave the way for other qualified officers to convert.

After a few days, I compiled my application, submitted it, and received my interview date and time. I scheduled one-on-one meetings with each of the ESO career service board members to ensure they knew who I was, my motivation, and the value I would add. About two weeks later, I had my 30-minute interview in a small conference room in the Operations Center, my home from five years prior. I had done my research and prepared thoroughly, so the questions were what I expected, and my answers were succinct and well-structured. At the end of the interview, I thanked the interviewers, shook their hands, and departed feeling good.

In February 2016, I received a phone call from Reynold, the deputy director of OPA, who was also a member of the ESO career service board and selection committee. "Parker, I just wanted to say congratulations. Welcome to the Executive Staff Officer career service." I smiled. A rush of positive energy came over me. Those words, "Welcome to the Executive Staff Officer career service," were all I needed to hear. I don't know if Reynold said anything else because I was too excited. I thanked him and told him I appreciated the board's support. I hung up the phone and walked to Stacey's office. I leaned against the door jamb and knocked on the door. She looked up at me, and I gave a slight smile and head nod. She smiled back. She already heard the news. "Congratulations, Parker. Go celebrate."

I took the rest of the day off. Never again would I have a group of analytic managers I didn't know telling me what was in my best interest. I knew what was in my best interest, and this accomplishment got me one step closer. When I returned to work the next day, the head of the ESO career service sent an email announcing the new ESO officers, and I received several supportive emails from friends and colleagues congratulating me on my accomplishment.

Now with my fate more in my own hands, I reached out to Preston to tell him the news. "Preston, I'm in the ESO! I know it has been some time since the vacancy last year, but I'm finally able to make the switch."

"I'm sorry, Parker," he wrote back. "We couldn't wait and already filled the position." It had been six months since I applied to be his deputy, and I understood that they couldn't wait for me. Betsy and the other managers offered it to someone else after three months. Preston and Betsy were still eager to have me join the team, in one capacity or another, and I was as motivated as ever to make that happen. We just had to wait, again.

My two years in OPA was ending, and I was encouraged by several managers to find a new position, as most officers in the ESO career service stayed in jobs for about 24 months. As I looked, I had one major goal in mind: what could I do to get closer to Preston and his team? I found a position in the newly created Talent Center, the office in the CIA that oversaw recruitment, human resources, diversity and inclusion, learning and training, and most important to me, professional development. I knew the chief of the Talent Center's communications group, and she told me about an opening on her team. I applied, and because it was listed as a job in my new career service, the application and approval went smoothly. I joined the new team in May 2016. I was one step closer to working with Preston.

A few months later, I called Preston. "I've got an idea for another *Leadership Now!* course," I told him. Always the one to try something new, he was excited and intrigued. I told Preston about a leadership philosophy from a Manhattan-based company called NextJump, whose co-CEOs had spoken at the CIA's annual TEDx event earlier in the year. After the event, they invited a group of CIA officers, including me, to New York City to attend their company's leadership academy, a two-day program explaining how NextJump develops its employees' leadership skills.

"We can turn the lessons I learned from NextJump into a two-hour seminar to develop CIA employees' decision making, critical thinking, and self-awareness skills, as well as positively impact CIA's own workplace culture," I said. "It creates our own practice ground for officers to take chances and make mistakes, all while learning and practicing those critical leadership skills necessary for higher levels." Preston and I met a few weeks later to discuss it in person.

After determining the schedule of events for the seminar, the topics, and the group exercises, he was all in. "Parker, man, I love this. I can't wait to see it in action." Preston always let people run with ideas, so I wasn't surprised that he supported this venture. Nevertheless, I was thrilled that he thought my idea was good enough to put under his invention, the *Leadership Now!* program. I got to work on preparing the two-hour seminar, and consulting with Preston, other trained educators and facilitators, and online resources to generate the most effective course possible. I was excited to once again be one of Preston's *Leadership Now!* instructors, as in my presentation at his day-long seminar in 2015.

As I was developing my seminar through the end of 2016 and into 2017, I was assigned to work on a new project to assist a handful of senior officers in developing a strategy for an initiative they called "Lead from Where You Are." Considering I was developing my own seminar to help officers lead from where they were, I was happy to be a part of the working group. One of the group members was Steve, Preston's second-level supervisor and the chief of the Professional Development Group.

At the end of our first meeting, I walked out with him. "It's interesting that I'm part of this working group because I'm developing a two-hour *Leadership Now!* course focused on these very principles," I told him.

He stopped and turned to me. "You're running a *Leadership Now!* course?"

"Yes, sir, I am."

Steve looked at me pointedly. "Then how come you're not working for me?"

Internally, I laughed. *Oh, Steve,* I thought, *how I could take you on an eight-year journey and tell you every detail of my trials.* But that wouldn't do me any good. I smiled, focusing my mind on future possibilities and not past circumstances. "I'd love to, and I'd love to do it while working a part-time schedule," I said. I was looking to reduce my weekly hours to have more time to work on other projects, like this book and music for Truth Assassin.

He smiled. "Well, I'm looking to hire part-time officers. Let's talk more sometime."

When we met a few weeks later, we determined that Steve had a need that I could fill: strategic communications. Steve's group was full of program managers like Preston that ran a lot of top-notch, exciting, and sought-after leadership and professional development programs, but he didn't have anyone with experience to help effectively advertise and market those programs to the rest of the workforce. Based on my experience in OPA and the Talent Center, the experience he was seeking was something I could provide.

We hammered out the details of what my work in his office would look like, including my strategic communications work, as well as continuing to run the *Leadership Now!* course I created. Steve said he would create the position and list it in the ESO career service as soon as he could. That, however, was the one thing in the process that would need to be approved. Because Steve was creating a new position, we had to ensure that its responsibilities and competencies aligned with those of my career service because the ESO career service board would have to approve it.

To pave the way, I talked with Chuck, one of the ESO career service board members who was an experienced, senior-level officer I trusted. I had worked closely with him during the past year, and he had supported my application to join the ESO. When we met, I told him about the ups and downs of the past two years while trying to join the Professional Development Group. "I think that group will be a great fit for you. Just do me a favor and ensure the position's responsibilities align with the appropriate criteria," he said. "If you can do that, we won't have any issues approving the creation of the position."

After the meeting, I contacted the ESO career development officer and a senior human resources officer, who gave me guidance on how to craft the tenets of the position. I passed the information to Steve, who crafted the official vacancy announcement and sent it to the ESO career service board for approval. After about a month of patiently waiting, the board approved it.

"The vacancy is out!" Steve wrote to me in an email in late April 2017. I clicked on the link, and it was exactly what we agreed upon. "Strategic Communications Officer – Professional Development Group – Seeking an experienced officer to provide strategic communications support to the Professional Development Group on a part-time, 24-hour-per-week schedule. Applicants should have multiple years of experience with strategic, internal CIA communications, photography and video editing skills, and experience in leadership and professional development." I was the perfect fit, just as we had discussed. I wrote my qualifications statement and submitted my application.

Two weeks later, the vacancy closed, and I awaited a call from Steve for an interview, a formality in the process. About a week after the vacancy closed, Steve came to my office and pulled me aside. "Parker, can I speak with you for a moment?"

"Sure," I said, assuming he wanted to talk about scheduling an interview.

"I just wanted to say congratulations, and welcome to the Professional Development Group." He shook my hand and smiled. He didn't even need to interview me.

In that moment, I reflected on everything I'd been through in the past eight years. It wasn't just my application that earned me the new position, it was the years I had spent working with Preston developing multiple leadership courses building my knowledge and understanding of leadership and professional development. It was my three years of honing my strategic communications skills. It was my never-quit, never-give-up, never-stop mentality to work in his group that earned me that handshake. It was my strong desire to join the one place in the Agency that I knew was the right fit for me.

I smiled as a calm came over me. I didn't jump for joy. I didn't scream aloud. I didn't run through the hallways celebrating. This moment was enough. Eight and a half years after I met Preston, I'd finally be working with him, side by side. I thanked Steve for the opportunity and his support and told him I couldn't wait to start.

On Tuesday, July 25, 2017, exactly 10 years and two days since I first stepped onto the CIA headquarters compound as an Agency employee, I walked to the door of my new office, located at one of the Agency's outer buildings. I stepped up to the door and looked to the side of the badge scanner. "Welcome to the Professional Development Group – Suite 5000."

I grinned. I made it. I scanned my badge on the badge reader. The lock clicked as it disengaged. I pulled open the door, walked inside, and greeted my new colleagues as I walked past them. I knew many of the people in the office, either through working with them in the Talent Center or because of the work I had done with them directly during the past several years.

"We're so happy you're here, Parker!" one teammate said.

"It's about time!" another one yelled.

"It's so great to have you! We can't wait to put your expertise to work," I heard from a third.

I walked to my new desk, further down the corridor. My name card was already hung on the outside of the four-foot-high cubicle wall. I felt welcomed. I took off my backpack and sat down in my desk chair. I started to enter my username and password to log in and get to work when I heard someone walking toward my desk.

He had on his typical workplace attire, a plaid, button-down, long-sleeved shirt, black slacks, black shoes, and glasses—small rectangular lenses on wire frames. His short, blondish hair with a few strands of gray was combed to the side. He had a beaming smile. As he approached me, he didn't even stick out his hand. He gave me a bear hug. Preston only said five words. "What took you so long?"

Of the seven stories included in this book, rereading this story brings up a significant amount of emotion: the car accident, the repeated, passionate pleas to change offices, the denial of new opportunities based on nonsensical policies, and simply the fact that it took me nine years to get to the office I wanted to work in. There is no doubt that I learned a lot along the way:

No one has your best interest in mind more than you. Of all the nonsense in this story, the one instance where the insanity was most egregious was in the conversation I had with the three managers who told me they had my best interest in mind. I didn't know those people and had never worked for them. The only interest they had was their own. That mind-set may be fine for most people, but not people in supervisory positions. Leaders put their people first. Period.

Surround yourself with mentors, sponsors, and colleagues who support, care, and develop you. The relationship with Preston has been one of the most important relationships I have developed in my adult life. He's looked out for me, sponsored me, given me opportunities to succeed, partnered with me, and provided guidance on how to navigate the CIA. I've had other relationships with a select group of people that were as valuable, but there have been many more whose mentorship primarily served their own interests. Keep a keen eye out for these people and stay away. Get with the people who truly support you.

When opportunity strikes, hit it. There were several opportunities in this story where I had to strike when the iron was hot, but the most important opportunity was the chance with Steve who asked me why I wasn't working for him after I told him I was developing the leadership class with Preston. I could have ruined the opportunity by complaining about all the times I tried to work in his office and how they didn't work out, but that would have done me no good and potentially given him a bad impression of me. Instead, I realized the opportunity I had to start a new relationship with a person who was able to shape my career path. I focused on the present, and capitalized on the opportunity.

Never give up. Never stop. Never quit. Get after it. It took me nine years following my recognition and decision that the CIA's Professional Development Group was the right fit for me to finally work there. It was an excessively long time for something that should have been so simple. It should have been so much easier. But it wasn't. And because it wasn't, I might not have learned all these lessons and I might not be the person I am today. In the end, as I look back, I had a goal and I was determined to get it. Yes, that determination may have wavered at times, and it might not have been constantly at the forefront of my mind, but it was always there. I always came back to it. It took me nine years, but I never stopped, I never quit, and I never gave up. It took me nine years to get after it, and I did it.

AFTERWORD: WHAT'S NEXT?

Chris Savos, a friend, colleague, and the first group-level manager I had at the CIA in 2007, was one of the first people (besides my wife Abby) to read a final, comprehensive draft of this book. When he finished, he said to me, "You make my life seem boring, and I'm almost twice your age." Chris was hyperbolizing, of course, as I think he has done equally amazing things in his life, but I'll admit that there was an ounce of truth in his words, and it made me realize how grateful I am to have had these experiences.

Yes, there were the times when I caused a car accident, almost triggered an interagency incident in Afghanistan, or had levels of stress that could have ended in a stomach ulcer. But at the same time, the lessons I've learned have benefited me greatly and have made me the person I am today. I'm sure you can tell from reading these stories that life, to me, is about getting after it. It's about continuing to work toward the goals and dreams that we know will make us happy, while implementing the lessons we learn from our own stories, as well as the experiences of others, to make those goals and dreams that much more attainable.

So where do I go from here? I keep going. I don't stop, I don't quit, and I don't give up. Now that this book has been published, I'll write another, and I've got several ideas already in the works on topics like funny stories from my world travels and the impact of the

Sitar Arts Center. Simultaneously to editing this book, I released a three-song EP for Truth Assassin called *Stuck in the Sand Trap,* and I continue to write music whenever I get an idea. I continue to hone my leadership and briefing best practices seminars and provide them to interested groups. I pitched small businesses from Washington, D.C. to New York City to let me run their internal communications on an ad-hoc and retainer basis. I advertised my photography skills to take pictures of local families. I created my limited liability corporation to house all these activities (and hopefully keep the IRS off of my back).

When people ask me, "Parker, how do you have this much time?" I respond with a simple answer: "I have just as much time as everybody else. It's all about how you use it." I understand my words are not profound, but it's what works for me, and maybe it could work for you, too. Our time on this earth is limited, and I'm committed to using each minute to the fullest, always getting better, spending time with loved ones, learning something new, giving back to my community, or creating something. And each time I do one of those things, I think back to the lessons contained in this book, committing myself to do everything I can and to *not* make the same mistake twice. It is inevitable that I will on occasion; it's human nature. But I control what I can, and always do my best.

In the end, that's what this book is all about: encouraging readers, whoever they are and wherever they may be, to be more successful in their own lives through motivating, inspiring stories and sharing the lessons I learned along the way. For those of you who found the motivation and inspiration I was trying to impart: thank you, and best of luck in your quest of getting after it, whatever "it" is for you. For those of you who weren't motivated or inspired: thank you for reading and best of luck to you, as well, in your quest of getting after your "it."

Aim high. Fail often. Learn from your (and my) mistakes. Be all you can. Do all you can. Grow yourself. Inspire others. Change the world. Be motivated, prepared, and confident. But most importantly, get after it.